Using ICT in Primary Mathematics Teaching

Using ICT in
Primary Mathematics
Teaching

Mary Briggs and Alan Pritchard

Learning Matters

First published in 2002 by Learning Matters Ltd.

British Library Cataloguing in Publication Data
A CIP record for this book is available from the British Library.

ISBN 1 903300 41 X

Cover design by Topics – The Creative Partnership
Text design by Code 5 Design Associates Ltd
Project management by Deer Park Productions
Typeset by GCS, Leighton Buzzard
Printed and bound in Great Britan by Bell & Bain Ltd., Glasgow

Learning Matters Ltd
58 Wonford Road
Exeter EX2 4LQ
Tel: 01392 215560
Email: info@learningmatters.co.uk
www.learningmatters.co.uk

Contents

Introduction

About this book

This book has been written for both trainee teachers and qualified teachers who wish to develop their knowledge and understanding of how Information and Communication Technology (ICT) can be used effectively in teaching and learning primary mathematics. On all courses of initial teacher training in England and other parts of the UK, a secure knowledge and understanding of how to use ICT to support the teaching and learning of mathematics is required for the award of Qualified Teacher Status (QTS) or its equivalent. For Newly Qualified Teachers (NQTs), mentors, curriculum co-ordinators, classroom assistants and other professionals, this book will help in identifying aspects of ICT use in the teaching and learning of mathematics which require attention. It is also an excellent resource book to recommend to colleagues.

The features of this book include:

- pedagogical and professional knowledge and understanding for the effective teaching and learning of mathematics using ICT;
- the exploration of ICT in its widest possible uses;
- discussion to assist the reader in deciding whether or not it is appropriate to use ICT to support the learning objectives for the daily mathematics lesson;
- practical classroom examples;
- research summaries;
- activities;
- further reading and references.

Developing the use of ICT in the daily mathematics lesson is central to this book. The three key principles underpinning any decision to use ICT in the daily mathematics lesson are:

- ICT should enhance good mathematics teaching – it should only be used in lessons if it supports good practice in teaching mathematics;
- any decision about using ICT in a particular lesson or sequence of lessons must be directly related to the teaching and learning objectives for those lessons;
- ICT should be used if the teacher and/or children can achieve something more effectively with it than without it. (DfEE, 2000a, p17)

In order to help you develop these three key principles, this book should be used as part of your ongoing professional development and to support your additional reading in this area.

Chapter 1 sets the scene. It gives a historical perspective of the development of the use of ICT in the teaching and learning of mathematics, and begins to address the reasons why teachers should use ICT in their teaching. This is supported by reference to research in the area. Chapter 2 offers an opportunity to audit your skills and levels of confidence in the use of ICT. Chapter 3 provides a starting point for thinking about the use of computers in mathematics teaching and learning; the focus here is on practical suggestions. In Chapter 4 we move away from computers to look at the widest possible use of ICT in mathematics classrooms. Chapter 5 considers the co-ordinator's role and Chapter 6 offers a starting point for locating resources of different kinds to support you, from the initial audit to future developments in your teaching using ICT.

In using ICT to teach mathematics there are specific skills that teachers, trainees and others will need to acquire in order to use equipment. It is beyond the scope of this book to teach the use of computers and other equipment. References to websites and further reading will enable you the reader to acquire and practise the necessary skills. This book concentrates on the pedagogic issues.

FURTHER READING

DfEE (1999) *The National Numeracy Strategy: Framework for Teaching Mathematics*. London: DfEE.

DfES/TTA (2002) *Qualifying to Teach: Professional Standards for Qualified Teacher Status and Requirements for Initial Teacher Training*. London: DfES.

QCA (1999) *Early Learning Goals*. London: QCA.

1 Using ICT in primary mathematics teaching

This chapter sets the scene for the current developments in the use of ICT in schools today through a brief historical overview, before looking at the current implications for the teaching and learning of mathematics with ICT.

More than twenty years ago, when computers first began to appear in primary school classrooms, there seemed to be an unspoken belief that there was a strong and undeniable link between computers and mathematics. The reasons for this seem reasonably clear, and in retrospect it is not surprising that the link was made; there was a dearth of suitable software for schools, but much of what was available dealt with simple mathematical topics.

The government-backed Microelectronics Programme (MEP) supplied programs for primary schools when the first funded computers were introduced in the 1980s. Of the better programs from this source, many were written to provide mathematical activity, e.g. the program 'Shopping' set up a simple situation in which children could choose specific items to buy from a selection of shops, make decisions about what they could afford, while saving enough for the bus fare home. Thus the link between computer-supported teaching and mathematics, which existed in the minds of many, was reinforced. It is interesting to note here that the maths–computer link did a good deal to encourage many teachers, but it is probably true to say that the perception of computers as mathematical machines put off a far greater number of teachers.

The development of a knowledge base concerning computers and learning mathematics

As the use of computers in primary schools expanded, and both teachers and other interested professionals took a deeper and more critical look at the use of computers in schools, the knowledge base with respect to the useful and less useful approaches to using computers to support children's learning expanded. More importantly, the wealth of experience amongst teachers also grew. It would not be true to say that all teachers became avid computer users, indeed even now, after many years of government initiatives and training, there are many teachers who do not make use of computers in their teaching, let alone *effective* use. Recent research (NGfL/BECTa/DfES, 2001) has found that 'the extent of ICT use in the curriculum appears to be dependent on the individual teacher' and that 'pupils can have very different experiences across different schools and subjects'.

More recently there has been an acknowledgement that well planned use of particular computer applications can support and enhance children's learning in a range of subjects, including, naturally, mathematics. 'Teachers can raise levels of pupils' attainment when they use ICT to support their teaching in ... numeracy and have clear objectives' (Mosely et al, 1999). The teaching of computer skills is recognised as important, and in many schools lessons with computers means specific lessons where children are learning about computers and about specific pieces of software: 'primary schools are teaching ICT skills separately. At Key Stage 2 this seems to have a positive impact' (NGfL/BECTa/DfES, 2001). In other schools, computers are used to support subject-based learning objectives, and specific skills are taught as needed, to allow children to carry out operations in pursuit of wider learning in a range of subjects. Needless to say, in some schools the two approaches are combined: skills are taught separately and software is used to support children's learning in a range of other subjects.

It is a requirement of Initial Teacher Training courses in England that you have to be trained in, and be able to demonstrate the use of, ICT in the core subjects and your specialist subject, and that you must be able to exploit its potential. You need to be able to make judgements about when and when not to use ICT, to be able to evaluate different forms of ICT hardware and software, and become confident and competent in the use of ICT. The Expected Outcomes of the National Opportunities Fund ICT training for in-service teachers specify the same requirements.

Supporting learning in mathematics using computers

The National Council for Educational Technology (NCET is now the British Educational Communications Technology Agency, BECTa) defines five major opportunities which the use of ICT is able to provide in order to support learning in mathematics:

- learning from feedback;
- observing patterns;
- exploring data;
- teaching the computer;
- developing visual imagery. (NCET, 1997)

It is interesting to note that the use of a computer for repeated practice (drill and practice) is not considered to be of major significance. We will now consider each of these opportunities in turn.

Learning from feedback

When children are asked to carry out any sort of activity, they will expect and require some sort of feedback as part of the learning process. A computer can give impartial, non-judgmental feedback, and never tires of doing so. The feedback which is available when using a variety of programs, in conjunction with the facility to make changes extremely easily, encourages children to conjecture and hypothesise, to try out ideas and to use an approach which is both problem solving and risk taking.

Approaches that rely on trial and error depend heavily upon feedback. Certain computer uses, and also the use of calculators, are extremely well suited to providing feedback.

Observing patterns

Looking for and finding patterns in numbers and other mathematical situations is fundamental to, and essential for, the development of an understanding of many of the fundamentals of mathematics. The Programmes of Study for both Key Stages 1 and 2 outline the need to teach children about patterns in numbers and shapes, as illustrated in the following (QCA, 2000).

> Pupils should be taught to … create and describe number patterns; explore and record patterns related to addition and subtraction, and then patterns of multiples of 2, 5 and 10 explaining the patterns and using them to make predictions; recognise sequences, including odd and even numbers to 30 then beyond; recognise the relationship between halving and doubling.
>
> *Key Stage 1: 2(b)*

> Pupils should be taught to … recognise and describe number patterns, including two- and three-digit multiples of 2, 5 or 10, recognising their patterns and using these to make predictions; make general statements, using words to describe a functional relationship, and test these; recognise prime numbers to 20 and square numbers up to 10 x 10; find factor pairs and all the prime factors of any two-digit integer.
>
> *Key Stage 2: 2(b)*

In the Key Objectives of the National Numeracy Strategy (NNS) (DfEE, 1999) the recognition and recreation of simple patterns is listed for Reception, and in successive years great reliance is placed on the use of patterns to help carry out arithmetical operations and solve all types of mathematical problems. Computer programs, either specifically written for the purpose of exploring patterns or a spreadsheet set up for the purpose, are ideal for this sort of work.

Exploring data

Using real data in examples for children to work with always used to be problematic. If numbers have to be manipulated without recourse to technology, then it is sensible to, first, keep the numbers simple, preferably whole, and secondly, to keep the number of examples to a minimum. ICT eliminates this problem.

A calculator or, even better, a spreadsheet allows for arithmetic, using real numerical data, to be carried out swiftly and accurately, and as many times as is needed. Spreadsheets can be configured to give only a manageable or appropriate number of decimal places, or significant figures, as required. Real data collected from real situations gives a meaning to the work, which somebody else's contrived or remote data does not.

RESEARCH SUMMARY

Pratt (1995) describes the graphing work of eight- and nine-year-old children, who have immediate and continuous access to portable computers across the whole curriculum. The children used the computers to generate graphs and charts from experimental data. He draws out two distinct uses of the graphing facilities available in spreadsheet software.

Passive graphing

Passive graphing is where the children use a graph to display the results at the end of an experiment and consequently the children come to see the graph as a presentational tool. The children using this approach made only pseudo-mathematical connections between the graph and the data.

Active graphing

Active graphing is where the children use the graphs to help them decide on the next action to be taken in the experiment. They are encouraged to generate the graph after the collection of only a few pieces of data; as they continue to collect data more graphs are drawn and interpretations made. The children are using the graphing as a meaningful and relevant tool: 'The child who sees graphing as an analytical instrumental has made a powerful mathematical connection which has fundamentally widened that child's grasp of the utility of graphing' (Pratt, 1995, p 165).

Pratt suggests that children encouraged to use the active graphing approach may be in a strong position to make further connections with an algebraic modality.

Teaching the computer

Seymour Papert, responsible for the development of Logo, believes that children should be in control when learning and, in particular, when using computers. He recommends that children should program computers rather than the computer programming the children. In Logo, Papert uses a teaching analogy to explain how children develop short pieces of program which, when run, will carry out a particular operation—draw a square, for example. In order that the computer be taught to draw the square, the child has to write instructions that are clear and unambiguous. Children thus take on responsibility for their own work and actions in this environment and are encouraged to take risks and to experiment. Naturally, the expectation is not that children are left alone with Logo and attempt to learn alone, but the context in which they work, with appropriate supervision and 'scaffolding', is centred on the children making decisions.

The need to teach the computer to carry out particular tasks leads to the need for children to develop their thinking, and to ask questions about shapes, numbers, arithmetic, algebra and sequence. A spreadsheet in need of a formula presents the child with a very similar situation.

For a full treatment of the use of Logo and of Papert's view on computers and learning see Papert (1980; 1993).

Developing visual imagery

In most cases, children benefit from some visual element in their learning. The proverb about hearing and forgetting, seeing and remembering, and doing and understanding comes to mind here. For example, if children are able to see shapes, build them and carry out transformations of them on a computer screen, they then take these images and construct their own knowledge of shapes. It is most likely that they will come to a deeper understanding of shapes and their relationships to each other than if they had only experienced a static version of the same phenomena.

There is obvious overlap between these areas of opportunity – for example, visual imagery, teaching computer use and feedback can take place at the same time in some mathematical learning situations.

RESEARCH SUMMARY

Gray and Pitta (1997) looked at using the resource of a graphical calculator to stimulate the construction of mental imagery associated directly with arithmetical symbols as opposed to imagery that is an analogical transformation of them. The imagery of 'high achievers' tended to be symbolic and was used to support the production of known and derived facts. The 'lower achievers' tended to be analogical representations of physical objects. The article describes Emily, a 'low achiever' working with a graphical calculator to change her imagery. The results suggested that Emily was building a different range of meanings associated with numbers and numerical symbolism as a result of the program developed for use with the calculator. She was moving away from a reliance on counting procedures.

Making use of ICT in mathematics

The Teacher Training Agency (TTA), which is the official body responsible for overseeing teacher training in England and Wales, has produced guidance for trainee teachers in respect of the standards that need to be achieved if QTS is to be awarded. This guidance is of equal use to teachers who are already qualified and who are seeking to develop their use of ICT in the classroom. Part of this guidance offers a rationale for making use of ICT in support of children's learning in mathematics.

All primary trainees need to know that ICT has the potential to make a significant contribution to their pupils' learning in mathematics, since it can help pupils to:

- *practise and consolidate number skills;*
- *explore, describe and explain number patterns;*
- *take their first steps in mathematical modelling by exploring, interpreting and explaining patterns in data;*
- *experiment with and discuss patterns in number and shape and space;*
- *develop logical thinking and learn from immediate feedback;*

- make connections within and across areas of mathematics;
- develop mental imagery;
- write simple procedures.

TTA (1999)

We will now look at each point of this rationale in turn.

Practising and consolidating number skills

Having rapid and easy access to basic operations – addition, subtraction, multiplication and division – is extremely useful for anyone dealing with numbers, both learners and more experienced users. Many teachers see the acquisition of these number operations as crucial to children's learning. The NNS places great importance on a mental facility with numbers and, understandably, there is a good deal of time spent in mathematics lessons working towards learning in this area. There are many items of software designed specifically for this purpose, some good, and some not so good. Some are presented in the form of a game or a challenge of some sort. Others allow for a measure of individual record keeping – this feature is sometimes very useful if work is to be individualised and offered at an appropriate level of difficulty, or if some additional practice with particular numbers or skills is to be either skipped, or offered when needed. Using software in this area of work in number is not the only approach that is useful and successful, and you must decide when and when not to make use of this option.

Exploring, describing and explaining number patterns

Working with number patterns, seeking and developing patterns and attempting to explain them is an important part of mathematics education. Traditionally this work has been covered in a number of ways – with the use of number lines and number squares, and more recently with calculators. ICT offers ways of giving speedy access to patterns and pattern generation, which can, in some cases, allow for more time to concentrate on the patterns themselves. There are simple programs which can 'count' in steps of different sizes or work with number lines and patterns in a more dynamic way than is possible on paper. Other 'content-free' programs, such as spreadsheets, give great flexibility to teachers and learners alike to set rules for the generation of patterns. In turn, this can lead into some of the ideas involved in algebra and the manipulation of numbers and variables.

Taking first steps in mathematical modelling by exploring, interpreting and explaining patterns in data

Simple graphing programs can, almost instantaneously, present a graphical model of collected data. The resulting pictorial model of the numbers can then be the focus of interpretation and analysis and a tool for explanation of the patterns, trends and anomalies that may be present in the data. More advanced modelling software, either for specific purposes (for example, a mathematical adventure game or a mathematical model of population growth) or for general purposes (for example, a spreadsheet) can be used to consider more complex representations of mathematical situations in a relatively simple environment which allows for changes to be made to the variable which make up the model, or to the 'rules' which control it.

Experimenting with and discussing patterns in number and shape and space

Under this heading it is possible to consider software which can first allow children to experience a visual representation of a particular phenomenon – fractions being formed from a larger whole, or triangles moving together in a way which seeks to show how to find the area of one of them – and then using the software to experiment and develop further ideas related to the work in hand. There are programs that allow users great flexibility in manipulating shapes and numbers in a free and yet at the same time controlled – by the rules of, say, geometry – environment.

Developing logical thinking and learning from immediate feedback

Working with binary (branching) data-handling software as a constructor, rather than as a user, puts an onus on children to think very carefully and logically about the sort of questions to consider when setting up a file. Young children would have to consider questions related to simple attributes – perhaps colour, size and shape; older children would have to consider more sophisticated notions – perhaps divisibility by particular numbers, or possibly something not related directly to mathematics, such as a particular creature's dentition or diet. The use of programmable toys or on-screen programmable objects is a very good example of children working in an environment which calls for a logical approach and which will also provide rapid feedback.

Making connections within and across areas of mathematics

A very good example of this idea for older children is a graphing program, or perhaps a spreadsheet, used to illustrate the connection between a line on a graph and the algebraic expression which underlies it. This is something which is not always easy for children to grasp, and the use of software alongside other activities and explanations is a very good way to help their understanding. The dynamics of a graph that responds to changes of numbers or perhaps the + or – sign can give instant feedback and aid understanding in a way that the laborious re-plotting of a graph on paper might not.

Developing mental imagery

This idea is closely connected to the idea of developing visual imagery. Enabling children to see something happen, either by their own doing – as a result of programming, or as a dynamic demonstration – will support the formation of mental images which will, in turn, assist in the process of coming to understand a particular phenomenon.

Writing simple procedures

There are fairly obvious overlaps here with the encouragement of logical thought and the use of immediate feedback, and with the notion that children can teach a computer as opposed to the computer teaching the child. Young children gain an enormous amount from giving instructions to a robot and seeing them put into practice successfully. This is something that is enormously satisfying for the children, and at the same time encourages the use of logical thinking and engagement with numbers. Older, more able children can experience the same sense of success and a higher level of engagement by working to complete other tasks and to solve other problems, which may often be of their own design.

ICT in classroom administration

The TTA outline the ways in which the use of ICT can enhance the teacher's wider professional role in relation to the teaching of mathematics.

> ... ICT has the potential to offer valuable support to the teacher of primary mathematics by:
>
> • helping in the preparation of teaching materials;
> • providing a flexible and time-saving resource that can be used in different ways at different times without repetition of the teacher's input;
> • providing a means by which subject and pedagogical knowledge can be improved and kept up to date;
> • aiding record-keeping and reporting.

TTA (1999)

Current progress

Recent official evidence of the progress being made in schools with the use of ICT in the teaching of mathematics can be gathered from two different reports from the Office for Standards in Education (OFSTED). The first one, which considers inspection data from 2001/2002 (OFSTED, 2002), makes the stark announcement that 'the good use of ICT to support mathematics is a relatively rare occurrence'. The second, an OFSTED evaluation report on the second year of the National Numeracy Strategy (OFSTED, 2001), says that 'To build on the progress made so far, schools should build on teachers' ICT training and the resources which are now in place to develop the use of ICT within the daily mathematics lesson, making further use of ICT training materials already published by the strategy'.

It is interesting also to refer to a Qualifications and Curriculum Authority (QCA) leaflet of January 2002 (QCA, 2002). The leaflet provides information on the implications for teaching and learning drawn from an analysis of children's performances in the 2001 National Tests at Key Stage 2. There is no direct mention of any implications for teaching that relate to the use of ICT. This is because there is no use made of ICT in the testing process except in its wider interpretation, which includes the use of a calculator. Testing the use of computers in the context of mathematics is perhaps something that will take place some time in the future.

✔ *Summary of key points*

- There is a tradition of connecting the educational use of computers with mathematics.
- There are well-defined areas of mathematical activity in teaching and learning which can be very well supported by the prudent and well-planned use of appropriate computer-based work. These areas of development in teaching and learning range from the straightforward use of the computer for practising and reinforcing number facts, to the more elusive idea of visual and mental imagery.
- Other valuable uses of advanced technology include work that could not easily be undertaken without a computer, at least not to the satisfaction of most – programming, or 'teaching the computer'.
- A recent comment is of interest: 'One of the paradoxes with which we have been grappling ... is why a technology whose founding fathers were predominantly gifted mathematicians should have so little effect in improving the numeracy skills of young pupils, so far at any rate.' (Fox et al, 2000, p139)
- The use of ICT in mathematics lessons is increasing, but it is still the case that the single largest use of ICT in primary schools, and probably also in the world at large, is word processing.

FURTHER READING

Cook, D. and Findlayson, H. (1999) *Interactive Children, Communicative Teaching.* Buckingham: Open University Press.

Monteith, M. (ed.) (1998) *IT for Learning Enhancement.* Exeter: Intellect.

2 Self-evaluation of needs

This chapter will enable you to audit your current skills and refer to the requirements set out in *Qualifying to Teach: Professional Standards for Qualfied Teacher Status* (DfES/TTA, 2002). It is these Standards that trainee teachers need to demonstrate in order to gain Qualified Teacher Status (QTS). However, these Standards, and this self-evaluation exercise, are also an excellent guide for established teachers focusing on the use of ICT in mathematics teaching and learning.

Self audit of ICT skills with particular reference to software relevant to the teaching of mathematics

You should be familiar with the following areas of ICT use. If you are a newly trained teacher you may wish to be updating your skills as part of your NOF training. You will be looking at your current level of skills and completing a needs analysis. Some of the skills below are generic and have applications across the range of computer use for teaching and the teacher's professional role; others are more specifically related to the teaching of mathematics. Some of the most general skills and processes have been omitted intentionally, such as the most basic of generic skills related to the very common uses of ICT, for example, basic word processing, printing, cutting and pasting and the simple saving and loading of files. Technical and trouble-shooting skills have also been omitted here.

Complete a copy of each of the following grids by ticking the appropriate column according to this key.

1. Competent – could easily teach a colleague how to do this.

2. Reasonably competent.

3. Little or no experience, therefore in need of development/support.

Spreadsheets	1	2	3
Enter numeric data			
Sort data in columns numerically			
Insert simple formula			
Copy formula from one cell to a selection of cells			
Create graphs and charts			

Databases (including branching/tree databases)	1	2	3
Set up a new data file structure			
Insert a new record/field			
Interrogate file to answer specific questions			
Create graphs and charts			
Add new items to a branching database			

Logo	1	2	3
Move screen 'turtle' around screen ('direct drive')			
Write a simple procedure, e.g. for drawing a square			
Use the 'editor' to create and modify procedures			
Write a 'compound' procedure – using other procedures			
Solve a problem using a large set of different procedures			

Internet	1	2	3
Make use of the Virtual Teachers' Centre to find resources			
Search widely for, and 'bookmark', relevant websites			
Find and use online resources			
Find and download programs and other resources			
Save images from websites to use in teaching resources			

Software	1	2	3
Aware of a range of practice and reinforcement software			
Aware of a range of topic-based software (e.g. DfEE CDs)			
Aware of a range of problem-solving software			
Install and run software – from disc, CD, website			

Self audit of ICT skills with particular reference to the teaching of mathematics

Here again you will need to make a judgement about your skills and experiences of using ICT in teaching and learning mathematics. For trainee teachers, the relevant standards for the award of QTS are stated at the top of the grids.

2.5 Knowledge and understanding

They know how to use ICT effectively, both to teach and to support their wider professional role.

Know how to use ICT to support planning and preparation of numeracy lessons	1	2	3
Understand and use the specialist terms associated with ICT used in mathematics, e.g. the use of appropriate terminology and specific skills			
Use a template for medium-term, weekly and daily planning as appropriate			
Know how to use ICT to support the monitoring and assessment of teaching and learning in mathematics, e.g. setting up assessment records to inform future planning			
Use templates for mathematical vocabulary			
Know how to use ICT to communicate and exchange ideas, e.g. discussion groups on the Internet, networking through email			
Know how to access government websites to update information about both mathematics teaching and learning and ICT, e.g. DfES Standards website			
Make OHP sheets using Word or PowerPoint templates			
Use PowerPoint for preparing materials to use in teaching mathematics			
Format reports to parents and governors, or policy documents for different audiences			

3.1 Teaching: Planning, expectations and targets

Know how to use ICT in teaching and learning mathematics	1	2	3
Know how and why ICT will be used to achieve the teaching and learning objectives			
Know when the use of ICT is beneficial to achieve the teaching objectives, and when it is not, e.g. images could be presented more clearly using other equipment			
Know what key questions and ideas need to be considered to ensure appropriate intervention in order to focus and extend children's learning, e.g. the difference in focus between passive and active graphing (see Chapter 1 p6)			
Recognise what resources are appropriate for particular tasks and children, e.g. overhead calculator, specific web sites, whiteboard and roamer			
Know how ICT can make a specific contribution to teaching children with special educational needs, e.g. touch screen, concept keyboard, enlarged print			
Know how to choose and use the most suitable ICT to meet teaching objectives through the selection of specific tasks and activities to enable children to achieve the objectives, e.g. developing number or counter to focus on understanding the whole number system			
Know how to contribute to the development and consolidation of children's ICT capabilities, e.g. the use of appropriate terminology, specific skills such as using spreadsheets and databases			

3.1 Teaching: planning, expectations and targets (continued)

Know how to use ICT and recognise its impact on the organisation of the lesson and the benefits of employing specific strategies in teaching and learning mathematics	1	2	3
Know how to introduce a topic to the whole class in the introduction to the main activity phase of the lesson using ICT, e.g. interactive whiteboard or single computer or overhead projector			
Know how to make use of group, paired and individual work to ensure children are engaged on tasks related to the learning objectives, e.g. some of these may use the computer and/or calculator			
Know how to allow access to ICT resources as part of planned and spontaneous need, e.g. as a way of dealing with large numbers in order to focus on the underlying mathematics rather than the calculations			
Recognise the most effective organisation of ICT resources to meet the mathematics objectives, e.g. use of suite or single computer; knowing which children will have access to the equipment			
Recognise opportunities for making use of equipment to its best advantage, e.g. digital cameras, overhead projector, tape recorders			
Monitor the teaching in a suite to ensure effective learning for all			
Recognise when to make use of support staff to assist children with ICT tasks in mathematics lessons and how this will affect the teaching and learning possibilities			
Know about health and safety issues, e.g. glare on screens, amount of time spent at computer			

3.2 Teaching: monitoring and assessment

Know when using ICT in mathematics lessons how to identify opportunities to monitor and assess children	1	2	3
Know which assessment criteria, based upon the teaching and learning objectives, you will use in the lesson in order to judge progress and attainment			
Know when to intervene to question and support children in terms of their mathematics and their ICT			
Ensure you can assess the mathematics and not just the ICT skills and knowledge, e.g. assessment of knowledge of number patterns rather than the use of the spreadsheet			
Recognise how you can assess children individually even when they are working in a group, e.g. will you ask individuals for a summary of their work, expect individual recording, question children?			
Know how the use of ICT can support the identification of the more able children and then extend their learning as part of on-going assessment			

Evaluating the audit

You have now completed your self-assessment audit. You may find it helpful to consider the two parts of the audit separately as your skills and experiences may be different in each section.

For the first part
- Mainly 1s means that you have more than the required personal skills in order to use ICT to support mathematics teaching and learning.
- Mainly 2s also means that you have the required personal skills in order to use ICT to support mathematics teaching and learning.
- Mainly 3s means that you have some of the required personal skills in order to use ICT to support mathematics teaching and learning, although there are likely to be some specific areas which you will need to develop.

When you have decided upon the areas you wish to develop for this part of the audit, you will need to plan for time to work on the specific skills and knowledge required. The list of books in the subject knowledge section of Chapter 6, pp 56–57 plus the help menus within the programs, will assist you in this task. Alternatively if you are a trainee, you can access help at any drop-in session held at your training institution.

For the second part
- Mainly 1s means that you are more than competent to prepare, plan and teach using ICT to support the teaching and learning of mathematics.

- Mainly 2s means that you are competent to prepare, plan and teach using ICT to support the teaching and learning of mathematics although there may be areas that you wish to develop further given greater opportunities.

- Mainly 3s means that you have some of the competencies required in order to use ICT to support mathematics teaching and learning although there are likely to be some specific areas, which you will need to develop.

In planning your actions in response to this part of the audit you may well find reading the rest of this book a good initial starting point before moving onto looking at specific areas. You can begin to look at specific areas by consulting the teaching resources section in Chapter 6, pp 57–58.

ACTIVITY

Carry out the audit as above and draw up an action plan in order to move all categories of skills and knowledge to at least a 2. You may find it helpful to organise your plan using the following template.

Action plan

Area of of focus	Date started	Date of review	Resources required	Training opportunities in school	Support from other people	Reading required	Any other issues
1.							
2.							
3.							
4.							

It is better to focus on a small number of items at a time and to plan when you will be able to work on them. Decide which can be achieved outside school and which have to be undertaken in school.

✓ Summary of key points

You have now assessed your ICT skills and set up an individual action plan for ICT and mathematics. This can be used, if you are a trainee, as part of your training plan, particularly when you are on school placement, or, if you are an NQT or an experienced teacher, as the basis for negotiating for time to focus on ICT and mathematics as part of your ongoing training and development.

- **It is necessary to audit your personal skills, teaching skills and experience either in order to meet the Standards required for QTS, or as part of your ongoing professional development.**
- **There may be a difference between your personal skills and the opportunities you have had to put those into place when teaching.**

- It is necessary to produce an action or training plan to develop your skills.
- This is currently an area undergoing considerable transformation and therefore developments in terms of skills, but more particularly opportunities, may take time.

FURTHER READING

DfEE/QCA (1999) *The National Curriculum: Handbook for Primary Teachers in England*. London: DfEE.

TTA (1999) *Using Information and Communications Technology to Meet Teaching Objectives in Mathematics—Initial Teacher Training: Primary*. TTA: London.

Introduction

This chapter will provide an overview of the issues to consider when planning and teaching mathematics lessons that include the use of ICT. It will act as a guide rather than provide models that will match every teaching context or situation you find yourself in. The most important consideration when planning and teaching any lesson is the needs of the learners, and this will vary from class to class and from topic to topic. Another variable is your access to hardware and software. Computers are the most obvious use of ICT but can be the most difficult for you to think about in terms of planning. Many teachers feel that they have not gained sufficient experience from their own use of computers. This can be a problem, but can sometimes be overcome by drawing on the expertise of the children who often have more positive attitudes to using computers. The first issue is preparation and with computers this means being familiar with the software and hardware available.

Before we look at some of the ways in which the use of particular computer applications can be integrated into mathematics teaching in primary school classrooms, we need to consider the purposes of computer use in this context. We also need to consider the range and style of software that is available. First, let us look at the some of the teaching that takes place in mathematics lessons and then consider the possibilities for computer-based activities supporting the various purposes that are embodied in different teaching and learning activities.

Purposes of teaching

It is possible to split the purposes of teaching into three broad categories:

- to introduce new ideas – this could also involve new skills;
- to allow for practice – this could be practice with new concepts, practice of new skills, or both;
- to encourage and practise problem solving – this could be in making use of the children's acquired concepts and skills, or it could be revising or reinforcing those that they have previously learned.

It is perfectly possible to plan and introduce computer-related activities for children that fit into the three categories above, sometimes in combination.

Let us now look for a broad description of these elements that will provide a full account of the teaching of mathematics, and then consider the ways in which ICT-related activities can be used to support the different stages in the process. The National Numeracy Strategy (NNS) document is clear about what it calls *direct teaching* and tells us that good direct teaching is achieved by balancing the following elements.

- *Directing*: sharing your teaching objectives with the class.

- *Instructing*: giving well structured information.

- *Demonstrating*: showing, describing and modelling mathematics using appropriate resources and visual displays.

- *Explaining and illustrating*: giving accurate, well-paced explanations, and referring to previous work or methods.

- *Questioning and discussing*: questioning in ways that match the direction and pace of the lesson and ensure that all children take part.

- *Consolidating*: maximising opportunities to reinforce and develop what has been taught.

- *Evaluating children's responses*: identifying mistakes and using them as positive teaching points.

- *Summarising*: reviewing, both during and towards the end of a lesson, the mathematics that has been taught and what the children have learned.

ACTIVITY

Consider the most recent lesson that you have experienced, whether as an observer or as the teacher. Under each of the headings above make brief notes about any aspect of the lesson that fits the description of each element of teaching. It may well be that there is nothing to write under some of the headings – does this mean that it could not have been a successful lesson?

If we look a little further afield and into the past we find a similar, but not identical, description of the component parts of mathematics teaching.

Mathematics teaching at all levels should include opportunities for:

- exposition by the teacher;

- discussion between teacher and children and between children themselves;

- appropriate practical work;

- consolidation and practice of fundamental skills and routines;

- problem solving, including the application of mathematics to everyday situations;

- investigational work.

DES (1982) para. 243

How can ICT approaches help with the elements of teaching described above? If we consider these elements under the headings set out earlier, we will see some of the possibilities for supporting teaching and children's learning in mathematics which can be provided through the medium of ICT.

Introducing new ideas and new skills

There are many occasions when a whole class introduction or demonstration of a new idea or process can be the most appropriate teaching method. In many cases, there is an appropriate computer-based approach to this phase of teaching, which will serve the teacher well. In classrooms with access to the latest projection facilities, the use of the computer to demonstrate and stimulate ideas and discussion can be both straightforward and very effective. In less well-equipped classrooms, there are certain problems to be overcome, but the use of an extra-large monitor, a television screen, or even a standard-sized monitor with smaller groups of children, can be equally effective. Whether software for demonstration purposes is used with a whole class or with a smaller group, its purpose and the role of the teacher remain the same: 'Your role is to demonstrate, explain and question, stimulate discussion, invite predictions and interpretations of what is displayed' (NNS, p31).

ACTIVITY

Consider the introduction of subtraction involving tens and units needing decomposition, such as $81-57 =$ to a group of children in Year 3 (NNS, p45). There is software available to demonstrate dynamically the decomposition process using on-screen representations of structural apparatus (for example, Dienes, Multilink). This software can also be used by individual children or pairs/small groups. Think about how you would organise the phase of your lesson following the introductory demonstration. Make decisions about the use of the software, the use of the actual structural apparatus, how to record findings and how to organise a plenary session. Consider the balance between the use of the software and the use of the apparatus itself.

Practising and reinforcing

Computers are endlessly patient and they are also capable of providing feedback at an incredible speed. Together, these two functions create a very good environment for practice and reinforcement. By using a computer, children in Key Stages 1 and 2 can 'practise and consolidate their number skills: for example by using software designed to ... "teach" ... or practise a particular skill and give rapid assessment and feedback to you and them' (NNS, p31). This is not to say that the computer should provide an electronic text-book page full of sums to complete, nor is it the case that every child in a class will benefit from time spent rehearsing calculations, or recalling facts which are already well known. Software can provide carefully targeted practice of certain skills, and engagement with new concepts. Your role is to ensure that the work is carefully targeted and that the repetitious nature of this sort of work is not overdone in individual cases. It is quite possible that some drill and practice programs are very well suited to some children's specific learning needs. Often work of this nature is specified on a particular child's Individual Education Plan (IEP).

ACTIVITY

Spend some time working through a piece of software designed to give repeated practice and reinforcement in some basic skills. For this activity, consider the possible negative effects that might result from poor performance.

- Is it possible to give incorrect responses? (Some software simply will not allow incorrect answers to be entered, often with no reason given.)

- Is the result of a wrong answer accompanied by an unpleasant face on the screen, a loud 'raspberry' or something similar?

- Is the user obliged to register a score on a league table of results, which will be visible to subsequent users?

- Is it possible to receive any diagnostic feedback, for child or teacher?

- Is any teaching support offered when mistakes are made?

Problem-solving

As you will see in the following section, there are many notionally simple programs available that deal with one specific mathematical topic and that present activities which require children to use a variety of problem-solving approaches. This section also points to the use of content-free software, such as a spreadsheet, for problem solving. It is interesting here to note that solving a numerical problem which has a correct answer is not the same as approaching a mathematical problem. In the various areas of mathematics – number, shape and space, and so on – problems may have a variety of solutions and can be solved by following one of a number of different possible routes. By using a computer, children in Key Stages 1 and 2 can develop their mathematical vocabulary, logical thinking and problem solving skills by using a 'branching tree' computer program to sort shapes or numbers, or exploring a simple simulation to discover the mathematical relationship that underpins it (NNS, p31).

Types of software

Computer software is, naturally enough, designed with different purposes in mind. There are different methods of software classification. Some are simple, and other less so. One simple system of classification is that a computer program can either be a *tutor*, a *simulator* or a tool. It is not difficult to come to an understanding of these three categories. A tutor teaches something; a simulator puts the user in a different context of some sort, perhaps imaginary, or perhaps a construction of a real situation; and a tool is a means by which a job might be completed more easily.

Tutor

Software that acts as a tutor can vary greatly. The approach taken to the teaching is usually rooted in one or other of the traditions of learning theory. Some, for example, may take a behaviourist approach, where learning is considered to take place when the learner is *rewarded* for correct responses and *punished* (possibly with the display of a sad face or a suitable sound effect) when a response is not correct. This type of software is designed to be used repetitively, and can resemble a textbook of some kind where many examples are given for practice. The term *drill* and practice is sometimes used for this type of software. The underlying learning theory of other software can be quite different. That which takes a constructivist approach, in which the user is encouraged to explore and investigate, can also be described as a tutor, but it clearly has a very different approach to the drill and practice examples.

Simulator

Simulations also come in a variety of guises. There are those that simulate a particular mathematical concept or operation, and those that simulate real or imaginary situations with which the user is expected to engage. Adventure games are usually set in an exciting world where there are problems to solve on the way to a predetermined goal. A spreadsheet, as we shall see, can be used in a general way as a tool, but a spreadsheet can also be set up to simulate certain problem-solving situations, and in this way work as simulator. This is one example of how specific software might straddle the classification categories.

Tool

Software designated as a tool is usually, but not exclusively, content free. We will consider this a little later. Put simply, software in this category allows certain jobs such as writing, drawing, constructing graphs, communicating and others to be carried out more easily than without recourse to the software.

Another classification sets out four subdivisions:

- *instructional* is akin to a tutor;
- *revelatory* is akin to simulations;
- *conjectural* allows for experiment and investigation and the user can try things out and learn from the process – Logo is one example of this type of software;
- *emancipatory* is akin to a tool.

(Sewell, 1990, p30)

At a more fundamental level, and possibly at a more useful level for the time being, it is possible to classify most software as either *content free* or as *content specific*. Although this classification system is crude, it can be used here to illustrate an important point.

Content-free software

Content-free software, also referred to as generic software, does not have any specific content. It is possible to view content-free software as a tool with a specific, or sometimes a varied and multifaceted, job that it can undertake, but in no particular subject domain. A word processor is an obvious and ubiquitous example of content-free software. A word processor can effectively carry out many tasks connected with the presentation of text (and pictures and other digitised objects), but the topic of the writing is not constrained to any particular subject. A word processor is not constrained by any other rules; the purpose to which it is put is entirely a matter for the user – it is possible to write about anything at all. The same can be said for other types of software. A database can hold data on any topic that the user may choose. There are proprietory databases with particular purposes, dealing, for example, with hotel room bookings but, as a general principle, if a database exists then it is possible to collect information and, more importantly perhaps, structure the collected information in a manner to suit the user. Equally, a spreadsheet is not in the least constrained by content.

Examples of content-free software

- Drawing programs.
- Graphing programs.
- Searching programs, e.g. web browsers.
- Multimedia design (including webpage creation) programs.
- Desk-top publishing programs.
- Hypermedia programs.
- Logo – sometimes considered domain specific since it is viewed as being very mathematical in its nature. (However, others argue that as a language, which is what Logo is, it is content free since it is possible to create all kinds of different end products, including those which are text based, or presented as pictures, or even as music.)

Content-free software, most likely, but not exclusively, in the guise of a word processor, a database or a spreadsheet, is widely available and has the potential to support children's learning in mathematics.

Content-specific software

Software with a particular subject focus is also very common. There are many examples of programs that are specifically written to encourage the learning of particular mathematical topics. By learning we naturally refer to the ideas set out above – introducing ideas and skills, practising and reinforcing, and problem solving. It is also the case that some software is designed for testing, and there is perhaps a place for testing software in the repertoire of mathematically-based computer use. Some of the software available is particularly well suited as a tool for demonstrations and for introducing groups of children to new ideas.

Often the content-specific software is delivered as a part of a suite of programs. Software developers and publishers are able to take advantage of CD-ROM technology and are increasingly producing collections of very useful items for the primary mathematics classroom. Another interesting feature of the current situation with regard to this type of software is that some seemingly very old software is being re-invented and brought into the sphere of advanced computer systems with all of the advantages that this brings with it. For example, some software titles which were distributed over twenty years ago to primary schools taking delivery of their first computers have been updated to take advantage of the improved features of modern computers and are enjoying a much-deserved new lease of life. Some of the original Microelectronics Education Programme software, which was very popular with teachers, fell into disuse as successive generations of new and improved computers failed to accommodate it. By taking a fresh look at some of the simple ideas that were contained in some of the early programs, it has been possible to rewrite and repackage them, and they are now being used again with increased success. This is partly a result of the DfEE distributing a CD and teacher materials to support the use of ICT in mathematics teaching in primary schools, and partly a result of the demand from teachers for software to support specific areas of the curriculum. The suite of programs under the broad banner of SMILE is another example of software which was first introduced some years ago, but which has easily passed the test of time and has been updated as changes in technology have demanded. These programs were initially for secondary mathematics but now cover all ages (www.smilemathematics.co.uk).

The Internet

Another source of simple, well-focused but effective mathematical activities is the Internet. There are numerous sites that provide activities designed to encourage the introduction of ideas, the practice of skills and participation in problem solving (see Chapter 6). Some of the activities available are quite simply excellent; others have features that should be questioned. As with all resources, teachers have to make informed judgements as to their value. An example of a very clever piece of computer programming is a simple program that allows a protractor to be manipulated on screen and used to measure a series of angles. This is fine, but in almost all cases it would be far better to allow children to manipulate a real protractor measuring a variety of 'real' angles. The use of an on-screen protractor could be a useful motivator, and it could be useful for reinforcing and practising skills that have been introduced in a more practical way, but in this case, it is important to use equipment in a real rather than a virtual context. One exception to this is when focusing on children with special educational needs (SEN), when the computer could allow such children to do the same work as the rest of a class. A child who has difficulties in manipulating a protractor physically may benefit from using an on-screen protractor because a mouse may be easier to use allowing the development of the mathematical concepts despite physical limitations.

Levels of use

There are three levels at which you could use computers as part of the daily mathematics lesson. As you train or develop as a teacher, plan to try out each level of use in school in order to be able to evaluate when to use each.

- Class
- Group
- Individual

Teaching and learning at class level

Before starting to plan for a mathematics lesson using ICT, you will need to ask yourself some questions about its content; these follow on from the discussion in the first part of this chapter.

- First, would the objectives for the daily lesson be enhanced by the use of ICT and, in particular, by the use of computers?
- Do you want to use computers during each stage of the lesson or just for specific phases of a three-part lesson?
- How does the use of the computer enhance the activities you will present to the children?
- How will the computer presentation alter what you will offer the children to do?
- How will the use of ICT affect the assessment of the children's progress and attainment in mathematics?

The following are examples of how you might use computers during the three-part NNS daily mathematics lesson. They represent a starting point for you to think about planning for ICT in mathematics lessons, and about using programs that are easily accessible to all schools – you may have access to a much wider range of potential programs, which you will need to evaluate before use.

MENTAL/ORAL STARTER WITH THE WHOLE CLASS

The mental/oral starter is for the practice of skills emphasising rapid recall of number facts as well as mental calculation. The key objective is to involve the children in participating in this phase of the lesson. The pace is brisk and teaching is limited to checking how the children might have worked out the answers to specific questions. In planning, you need to consider the advantages and disadvantages of various ways of presenting material and eliciting responses.

One computer for the whole class to focus on

For all the children to be engaged with the task, they all need to see what is going on. In suites or classrooms it may be possible to project the image of the computer screen onto a larger screen, or to use a larger television screen to supplement the computer screen. If you have only a small computer screen, you may need to move children around so that all children can see at different times.

Why use a computer for the mental/oral part of the lesson? Visualisation could act as a prompt to children's thinking, particularly about number. It is helpful to many children to see another image of the numbers while completing a task. For example, a counting program, which could be set to count in jumps starting at a given number, can provide children with support as they see the program count in given steps. In addition, all the children will be able to take part. These programs can also be set up to stop, at which point you can ask the children what the next number will be in the sequence, thus offering opportunities for focused differentiated questions.

What might the disadvantages be of using this kind of activity in the mental/oral starter? The display of the numbers may be too small on the screen for everyone to see. It provides only one visual image for counting as the numbers are displayed one at a time and therefore not in relation to each other. Other equipment may actually offer more effective images for children to support specific objectives, such as counting sticks, number lines and/or number squares. Moreover, the pace is dependent upon the pace of the counting on the computer. This could be too slow or too fast depending upon the set-up menus available. Since you (the teacher) are using the program as a teaching tool it does not offer opportunities for children's progression in their ICT skills, as there would be limited hands-on experience during these activities.

Interactive whiteboard

Counting exercises, for example, could be done with an interactive whiteboard. This would allow more opportunity for the children to get involved as they can set the counting gaps and/ or input the responses to specific questions (see Chapter 4, p48). However, as with all equipment there are some practical points to consider before you can employ interactive whiteboards effectively to support teaching and learning. At the time of writing, they are relatively new pieces of equipment and many teachers will be unfamiliar with them. If the actual logistics of using the equipment is not an issue, there still remains the more difficult question of how to teach using one. Like any other boards, there are basic issues about monitoring the class and either writing or manipulating objects on the interactive whiteboard. In many suites, for example, the organisation of the room means that children are peering around large computer terminals in order to see. If this is the case, it may be possible to gather children together in front of the whiteboard during the mental/oral phase of the lesson before the children move to their main activity tasks either at their tables or computers.

Each child with a computer

In choosing to work with computers in the mental/oral phase of the lesson with the whole class, you will need to decide upon a specific activity. This activity could be for all the children at the same time, e.g. using 'Developing Number' software with the number complements (for example, numbers which make 10), or tables set against the clock. The 'Developing Number' software is available from the Association of Teachers of Mathematics (ATM) and it has the facility to set and track the progression of individuals against set targets and time, e.g. Year 3 NNS, p30/31, mental calculations -/+. Alternatively, you might present the task to all the children on individual computers but ask for oral responses rather than the children inputting their responses silently.

MAIN ACTIVITY WITH THE WHOLE CLASS

This part of the lesson is where the main direct teaching input includes explicit modelling and demonstration of specific strategies to be used in any subsequent activities. In this part of the lesson, the main issue is how you present the key ideas in order to encourage children's understanding (Year 5, NNS, p111). For example, if to understand and use angle measurements in degrees is the objective, you could use part of the angle program in the DfES Maths and ICT pack (DfEE, 2000a), which is also available from the Standards website (www.standards.dfee.gov.uk.numeracy). This angle program can be used to model how to use a protractor and also how to estimate the size of angles to the nearest 5°. This is one of the key objectives in Year 5.

One computer for the whole class

An example of this method of working can be seen in the *ICT in Mathematics* video (DfEE, 2000a), available from the DfES. One of the examples shown is a numeracy advisor using 'Developing Number' software, specifically the numbers part; demonstrating the making of three-digit numbers for the class and discussing each digit value. The children are using arrow cards as well as the images on the projected computer screen to support their visualisation of the numbers.

Interactive whiteboard

One of the NNS Year 2 objectives is for children to begin to understand division as grouping (as repeated subtraction) or as sharing (NNS, pp47–49). Using the 'Easi Teach' program (www.easiteach.com), you could set up large objects on the whiteboard that could be manipulated into groups to explicitly model the action of sharing. Not only could you model this, but with different groups of objects you could ask children to model this for the whole class. You could use a suite or a classroom for this activity depending upon the range of technology available at the school in which you are working.

Each child with a computer

In practice, most school computer suites do not yet have one computer per child. Therefore, the set-up is probably two or three children at each computer in a suite. In this case, you will need to consider the differentiation required. You may have chosen a program to use where the differentiation is by outcome with all children working on the same initial task. You could group the children according to ability and set up different levels of task, for example, by using the 'play train' from the DfEE CD-ROM (DfEE, 2000a). With this, it is possible to set a range of specific problems with different numbers.

A significant issue with using computers in this part of the lesson is the choice of software. Content-specific software is likely to have more limitations in terms of the range of differentiation it will allow for whereas content-free software is likely to be more flexible.

PLENARY SESSION WITH THE WHOLE CLASS

This part of the lesson is where the learning is reviewed against the shared objectives. Misconceptions and errors are rectified, if possible, in drawing the lesson to a close.

One computer for the whole class

You could ask a group to share what they have undertaken during the main part of the lesson if they have been working with a computer. This would involve sharing the activity, reporting any misconceptions and errors that occurred and perhaps also demonstrating to the rest of the class how a specific program is used so that others in the class are prepared for its use in future lessons.

Interactive whiteboard

The use of the whiteboard offers an opportunity to return to the key ideas demonstrated in the main activity and directly rectify any errors and misconceptions. It might also be an opportunity to reinforce ideas and perhaps plan a game (see, for example, NNS, Year 2, p15: order whole numbers to at least 100 and position them on a number line and 100 square). You could use 'Monty' from the DfEE pack (DfEE, 2000a) here. This is a number square with a snake called Monty who moves around the grid. You can stop Monty at any time so that he covers some of the numbers. You can then ask the children to discuss how they would work out what numbers are hidden by the snake's body and how they know. This would give children an opportunity to show you what they have learnt as they use the image of the number square on the computer. You can then assess their learning against the objectives.

Each child with a computer

When each child has a computer available during the plenary session, it is most likely to be in a suite environment, which means that the class has probably worked on computer activities during the other parts of the lesson. In this situation, you could arrange to show the work of one child or a small group of children on everyone's machine so that they could all focus on the same piece of work. Alternatively, you could just use the computers during a plenary session to extend the work completed in the classroom. If the rest of the lesson had focused on graphs and interpreting data, you could then move into the computer suite to look at graphical representations of data selected from different sources using Excel. These could be displayed on all the machines for a discussion of how the use of the computer changes the data interpretation, ease of reading scales, etc. (NNS, Year 4, pp114–117: organising and interpreting data, including that generated by computer.)

COMBINATION OF STARTER AND MAIN ACTIVITY WITH THE WHOLE CLASS

This could focus on two separate objectives, one for the mental/oral starter and one for the main activity phase, or alternatively it could focus on one objective covering both phases of the lesson.

One computer for the whole class

Separate objectives

- For the mental/oral starter (Year 6, pp78–81: reasoning and generalising about numbers) you could use a function machine from the DfEE pack (DfEE, 2000a) on the computer screen. This is a program where you set the machine to do 'something' to a number you input. It then gives you an output, e.g. if I put in '3' and the machine outputs '6', I may think it is adding 3. So to check, I put in '4', and the machine outputs '8', so I know that the machine is actually doubling the numbers (provided it is working in only one step). You might set the program to rapidly work out two-step functions from inputs and outputs.

- For the main activity phase of the lesson (Year 6, p111: shape and space – recognise and estimate angles and use a protractor) you could use 'Angle' (DfEE, 2000a), a program that offers a variety of different activities where children can estimate and measure angles on the screen.

Same objectives

One example of using the same objectives for both the mental/oral and main activity would be for a Year 1 class to describe and extend number sequences, and count on and back in steps of any size (NNS, p6). A choice of software could be used to support this objective. First you might start with a number square from the Ambleside school website (www.ambleside.schoolzone.co.uk/ambleweb/numeracy.htm) as a support to counting on and back, starting in different places and using different jumps. The counting could be oral, but with one number square as the focus of attention with you and/or the children pointing to the patterns created. In the main activity, the same site could be used to highlight specific patterns. Or you could change to a counter or a counting machine that will allow you to set up counting patterns that you can stop and ask the children to make predictions before they go on to work on number patterns of their own, away from the computer. Of course, one group could still remain working on the computer but this is not necessarily its most effective use.

Interactive whiteboard

The same programs could be used as above, but with the additional use of an interactive whiteboard, which would allow more interaction between the children and the computer program. The larger screen would also allow you to model more clearly (see Chapter 4, p48).

Each child with a computer

The first decision that you need to make here is whether you try to use the same program and activity for both the mental/oral and the main activity. This example uses different programs because of the differing expectations of each phase of the lesson. The mental/oral phase is characterised by a brisk start at a good pace. Therefore you need to choose something which encourages pace; alternatively the way you set up the activity could ensure that the pace is maintained. Examples of these alternatives would be either to set up a timed program such as 'Develop Number' to practise number facts, where the program allows you to set the time for each learner, or you might choose a program without a timing option and ask the questions yourself, keeping the pace brisk. You might, for instance, set up Monty with a challenging spiral grid.

The choice of main activity support will obviously depend upon your objectives for the lesson. If they are related to solving problems (covered in each year) you might choose a range of problems from the Ambleside school website (www.ambleside.schoolzone.co.uk.ambleweb/numeracy.htm) for individuals to work on.

COMBINATION OF MAIN ACTIVITY AND PLENARY WITH THE WHOLE CLASS

Computers can be used in the main activity for modelling in different ways and then for recapping on the objectives in the plenary.

One computer for the whole class

Here the computer needs to be seen by the whole class in order for it to effectively enhance the teaching and learning of objectives. For example, the 'Take Part' program (DfEE, 2000a), which shows conservation of fractions of the area of shapes in short sequences which change the images, could be used as an introduction to a lesson focusing on fractions. (NNS, Year 2, pp21, 23: begin to recognise and find one half and one quarter of shapes and small numbers of objects). The program offers the opportunity to see half of a square in different coloured patterns where the fraction of each colour remains the same. The main activity would need to include the modelling of halves of small quantities without using a computer. The class then moves to activities, which might include the children working on the program used in the first part of the lesson, or at www.bbc.co.uk/schools/numbertime/games/index.shtml, which focuses on different challenges. The plenary session may involve moving on to looking at quarters and thirds with 'Take Part', and therefore extending the learning.

Interactive whiteboard

You could use clock-face background resources on an interactive whiteboard for a class of Year 1 children (NNS, p78: measures — read the time to the hour and half hour on an analogue clock). Here the whiteboard could be use to model a clock and individuals could mark times on the clock faces before moving to more independent work away from the whiteboard. It would be a good idea to return to the same background resource during the plenary phase to recap on more examples, and perhaps introduce quarter past and quarter to the hour, so extending the learning in the lesson (see Chapter 4, p48).

Each child with a computer

That each child has a computer will influence your choice of activity. It means that the children can practise skills independently, so drill and practice software could be used here. Alternatively you may wish to set up specific challenges for children at three different levels, perhaps even using three different programs. However, the latter can be difficult to monitor if you have limited experience of the programs and/or of working with a class under these conditions.

The following is an extract from a lesson plan in which Year 4 children from a more able set used computers in groups of three during the main activity and the plenary.

Curriculum links	Learning objectives
NNS Y4 p114 Extension Y5 p115 NC maths KS2 Ma 2 1a, c, f, h Ma 41c, f, g 2a, b, c Breadth of study 1f ICT: KS2 1b, 2a,4b, c	By the end of the lesson: • all children should be able to find the answer to a problem by interpreting a bar chart with axes marked in multiples of 2 and 5; • most children should be able to construct a bar chart.

Teacher activity	Children's activity
Main activity	
Show the children a blank bar chart with spaces for labels. Ask the children if they know the names of the axes, labels, title and scale.	Suggesting names for different parts of the chart.
As they respond, write their suggestions for each in empty boxes, e.g. scale of 1, 2, 5 and 10.	Suggesting suitable examples for the labels, scale, etc.
Show children's 'birthday' bar chart and ask them questions based on the chart, e.g. what is the title, scale, etc.?	Looking at 'Happy Birthday' bar chart.
Ask the children questions based on data in the bar chart; explain how to read the scale.	Answering questions by looking at the graph.
Recap on previous work on collecting birthdays from the class.	
Explain main activity.	Groups of three: work on 'Handi Graph' program to construct a graph of Year 4's favourite pets from data collected, including title, labels and scale.
Focus on group 4 and 5 to begin with — may need help getting started.	
Ask groups questions based on graph, e.g. Which is most common pet, Which is the second least common pet, etc.?	Extension: try to construct the graph with a different scale. Which scale is easiest to read?
Plenary	
Look at horizontal bar charts.	Labelling the horizontal bar chart and asking questions they would like to answer based on the graph, e.g. How many pets do children in the class have altogether?
Explain that they are the same as vertical bar charts except the axes are the opposite way round, i.e. the scale is along the bottom rather than up the side.	

Look carefully and critically at the plan. How might you alter this from a passive graphing activity to an active one (see Chapter 1, p6)? What kinds of questions would you use to look more deeply at the data collected? For example, why is one pet the most common in Year 4? If computers were available, how could you access graphs from the Internet to compare yours with? Although this plan uses 'Handi Graph' software (which allows you to create blank graphs, grids and number lines in Microsoft Word — www.handigraph.com) the same kinds of activities could be planned using Excel.

Teaching and learning at group level

It is worth considering where you will target your attention during the main activity. Group work can assist you in providing further modelling for a group or groups after your direct teaching introduction. You might wish to set a different level of challenge for a more able group of children. Group work could also provide you with an opportunity to use 'probing questions' to assess children against specific objectives for a group. Your role during the main activities is important as you are a valuable resource to support learning. You therefore need to plan your input carefully. Remember, though, that if you are working with a group, you also need to be monitoring the learning of the rest of the class at the same time.

You may need to use group teaching during the other phases of the daily mathematics lesson as a result of a wide ability range in your class and/or a wide age range. For example, in a small rural school you may have all of Key Stage 2 together in one class. In order to address the children's needs, you may need to teach them in groups with the help of a teaching assistant.

USING A TEACHING ASSISTANT WITH A GROUP FOR A MENTAL/ORAL STARTER

Increasingly, teaching assistants are used to support individuals and groups within the daily mathematics lesson. ICT is just part of the equipment that these assistants might employ in their role. In order to carry out their role effectively, they will need details of how to use programs, questions to ask children and maybe even advice on assessment. You may find it useful to produce a guide, like the one on page 34, to support your teaching assistant in his/her work with children using ICT during the mathematics lesson.

TEACHING ASSISTANT GUIDANCE AND ASSESSMENT SHEET

Name of teacher: Class/set:

Date: Lesson focus: Mathematics and ICT

Name of classroom assistant/additional adult:

Activity:
Brief account of the activity and focus for support.

Key questions to ask when the children are working on the activity:

Mathematics and ICT specific vocabulary to use:

ICT resources to be used:

Key issues/operating instructions for using ICT resources:

Mathematics learning objectives: ICT learning objectives

1.   1.

2.   2.

3.   3.

For the assistant to complete.

Note: Difficulties/issues when planning

Children's names	Maths	Can do	Diff	ICT	Can do	Diff	Next level of support
	1			1			
	2			2			
	3			3			
	1			1			
	2			2			
	3			3			
	1			1			
	2			2			
	3			3			
	1			1			
	2			2			
	3			3			

One computer for the group

It is probable that the reason for using a computer with a teaching assistant and a small group is to differentiate more effectively for this specific group of children. The computer here offers the opportunity to provide additional visual support for the development of mental/oral skills. Depending upon your objectives, you may wish to choose number squares, number lines or other similar images to support the group. The group may be positioned in the classroom away from the rest of the class or outside the classroom. In the latter case, you will still need to monitor the group. You could make specific arrangements with another teacher about this, depending upon the physical set-up in the school.

Interactive whiteboard

For one group, you could use the interactive whiteboard to focus on writing numbers in figures and words and reading the numbers in the two forms. A prepared set of questions could be displayed as a Word document as the main task in the mental/oral phase of the lesson. Members of the group could then come up and write their answers on the whiteboard. The important decision to make is in relation to the needs of the group and the expected pace of this part of the lesson.

Each child with a computer

It is possible, where children have different needs, for each child to work on a different program. With many different programs, this might become unwieldy for the teaching assistant, but with a group of three children it could be managed if the teaching assistant is familiar with the programs. Children in such a group are more likely to be those who need additional support and therefore drill and practice programs; a short period, perhaps 5–10 minutes, could be very effective for them. The speed of the questions asked can be varied to suit the ability of the individual while the teaching assistant monitors the child's responses.

MAIN ACTIVITY WITH A GROUP WITHIN THE CLASS

A main activity for a group within the class could be part of the Springboard lessons for children in Years 3, 4 and 5. These are catch-up programmes for children who have been identified as achieving just below national expectations in each of these year groups (DfEE, 2000b, 2001a, b).

One computer for the group

An example of such an activity is 'Toyshop' in the DfEE/ICT pack (DfEE, 2000a) NNS, Year 2, p69: recognise coins and notes of different values and solve simple problems involving money. The computer is used during the main activity with a group and the teacher works with them. An obvious organisational issue is the kind of activity the rest of the class are given by the teacher in order that she can work with this group. In the video sequence the rest of the class are working on related activities. The whole class then work on the program with the computer during the plenary phase of the lesson.

Interactive whiteboard

One advantage to using an interactive whiteboard is the preprogrammed resource background that you can use, for example, a grid can be used for teaching about place value, labelled to emphasis the value of each digit (NNS, Year 4: p2 read, write whole numbers, and know what each digit represents). The grid can be used to model the written form of whole numbers whilst the children can make the numbers using arrow cards. Children can be asked to make numbers and to write them in the grid then move on to writing them without the grid.

Each child with a computer

Here a drill and practice program may be useful to support a small group working with a classroom assistant. Note, however, that a teaching assistant should not be asked to deal with a number of different programs at the same time alone (although this depends on their experience and familiarity with the programs). You may choose a program from a mathematics scheme to support the specific practice of objectives, or plan for a group to work with a specific program, such as Logo, at a slightly slower pace so that subsequently they can then work within the class as a whole.

Teaching and learning at individual level

A number of schools have decided to use integrated learning systems (ILS) for each individual child; they may, for example, have decided to target children who appear to be just under the achievement levels required for a specific National Curriculum Test level, at the end of Key Stage 2 in particular. If you are a trainee, you will need to ask if your placement school is using this approach to support a specific group of children on an individual basis. Systems can vary so you will need to find out the focus for mathematics and to establish when children are expected to complete their tasks on a computer, and how often, before progress is assessed and programs altered accordingly.

Using a teaching assistant with an individual during a daily mathematics lesson

The most common situation to consider here is the special needs teaching assistant who is specifically attached to an individual child as part of their SEN provision. There may be other times, however, when additional support is available and therefore it is important to consider how to use that support, including using ICT.

Children with special needs

SEN

There are a number of ways to consider the use of ICT to support SEN children. One way is to see ICT as allowing an individual or group of children to engage with the mathematical concepts that would otherwise be difficult for them to access in the same way as the rest of the class.

Another perspective is to see the use of ICT as supporting the repetition of basic skills that a child needs to practise on an individual or group basis. The kind of software that would fit into this category would be content-specific and could also include drill and practice activities. This view of the use of ICT could be applicable at any time, not just within the daily mathematics lesson. It could offer an opportunity for a child who may well be working below the attainment of the rest of the class to engage in independent work; their time might be planned as a series of short activities to keep them on task and motivated.

More able children

Although we tend to focus more on differentiation issues for lower ability groups and SEN children it is important not to lose sight of the needs of all children. You may be teaching a class where there are some very able children. These children are now referred to as gifted and talented (G and T).

If you are a trainee on placement, enquire; there may well be a specific policy in your placement school detailing the expectations for the support of such children.

There are a number of views that you might consider when working with able children.

- A computer may be seen as a tool to support the development of mathematical thinking generally, through the presentation of specific problems to solve, making use of existing skills, knowledge and understanding. For example, a database of information about the properties of shapes could be used to set up activities that focus on asking questions that allow children to demonstrate their understanding of shape classification.

- A computer may be seen as a tool to enable the extension of children's thinking in a specific area, e.g. the use of active graphing to interpret data handling results, which could take children beyond their abilities to draw the graphs by hand.

- A computer could be seen as a means of providing differentiated tasks from the class objective for an individual or group, e.g. a multiplication task may be expanded to include the use of larger numbers in the tables section of 'Developing Number' software. The complements could be set to focus on decimal numbers to two decimal places to provide a challenge at speed in Key Stage 2.

- A computer may be seen to provide the opportunity for an extended piece of mathematics over a series of lessons for a small group, e.g. using Logo to write procedures for tessellating shapes and combinations of shapes by building up procedures over a number of sessions, or to set up a specific challenge related to the class objectives but taking this group further. Again, there are opportunities for developing mathematical thinking through these activities.

✅ Summary of key points

- **A clear decision needs to be made about whether or not to use ICT as part of the teaching strategies for a lesson and why.**
- **There must be an awareness that the use of ICT will alter the teaching strategies and possibilities.**
- **There must be an awareness that the use of ICT will alter the learning that takes place.**
- **Careful consideration must be given to the appropriateness of the ICT to enhance the learning of the objectives for a lesson or sequence of lessons.**
- **Effective teaching strategies make appropriate use of ICT when it supports the progress of learning against the objectives.**
- **ICT can be used for a part of or the entire NNS three-part lesson.**
- **ICT can be used to support the whole class or groups and individuals within a daily mathematics lesson.**

- **Possibilities and constraints differ when working in the classroom with one or two computers and when teaching in a computer suite.**
- **Assessment of children's mathematics when using ICT needs to take account of the effects of the specific ICT employed, which may alter potential levels of attainment.**

FURTHER READING

DfEE (2000) *Guide for Your Professional Development: Using ICT to Support Mathematics in Primary Schools.* London: DfEE publications.

Fox, B., Montague-Smith, A., and Wilkes, S. (2000) *Using ICT in Primary Mathematics: Practices and Possibilities.* London: David Fulton.

Hayes, D. (2000) *Handbook for Newly Qualified Teachers: Meeting the Standards in Primary and Middle Schools.* London: David Fulton.

Jacques, K. and Hyland, R. (eds.) (2000) *Professional Studies: Primary Phase.* Exeter: Learning Matters.

Sharp, J., Potter, J., Allen, J. and Loveless, A. (2000) *Primary ICT: Knowledge, Understanding and Practice.* Exeter: Learning Matters.

4 Using other technologies in primary mathematics

Introduction

In this chapter we will look at a wide variety of ICT resources that can be employed in the daily mathematics lesson. In addition to computers, there is a range of hardware that can be used to set up and develop learning situations. There are often links between these types of hardware and computers, but they can often stand alone. You will usually use some of these technologies for demonstration and exposition, while the children may use some either alone or in small groups.

The use of non-computer technologies also has a cross-curricular dimension. In the course of introducing children to aspects of the National Curriculum for ICT it is quite likely that learning objectives across other subjects might be planned for and achieved. There are times when one element or another of the ICT Programme of Study coincides with elements of the Programme of Study of another subject. In ICT, for example, in the strands relating to both 'Developing ideas and making things happen' and 'Reviewing, modifying and evaluating work as it progresses' it is suggested that working with a programmable toy of some kind would be appropriate; this would also be appropriate for activities designed to help meet mathematical objectives.

ACTIVITY

Jot down all the things that you could use in the classroom when teaching mathematics that come under the umbrella of ICT.

The DfEE's guide to using ICT to support mathematics in primary schools (DfEE, 2000, pp19–20) offers the following suggestions:

- digital camera;
- floor robot;
- CD-ROM encyclopedia;
- pocket calculator;
- audio cassette recorder;
- computer programs;
- television broadcasts;
- the internet;
- interactive whiteboard;
- video camera;
- binary tree programs;
- sensors attached to a computer;
- flash movie;

- OHP calculator.

We are now going to consider the use of such items as:
- programmable robots;
- calculators;
- digital cameras;
- video cameras;
- television;
- audio recorders;
- overhead projectors;
- interactive whiteboards.

Programmable robots

The use of toys for supporting learning is not an idea that accompanied the advent of new technologies. However, the use of programmable toys that rely on microchip-based technology is relatively new. Twenty years ago a 'Big Trak', a battery-operated, tank-like toy, could be given a set of instructions for moving and turning. Children could attempt to give a set of instructions which, when implemented, would move the Big Trak from A to B via a predetermined route. This activity was valid then and is equally valid now. Similar technology has passed through incremental stages of development – dome-shaped 'turtles' connected by cable to a computer, then turtles in contact with the computer via an infra-red, remote-control style link, and most recently, and most successfully, totally independent floor robots of various shapes and sizes.

There is a strong connection between these toys and the development of Logo. The screen version of Logo evolved alongside the concrete, floor-robot version that uses the same language. The first triangular item to move around the Logo screen was, and often still is, referred to as a turtle.

The use of a floor robot is seen as a precursor to the use of Logo on the computer. It is true that young children seem to find it easier to begin to use Logo on the screen if they have had experience of the larger-scale version on the classroom floor. However, the use of a floor robot alone is a very useful means of introducing children to a range of mathematical concepts. An insight into the philosophy of Logo would allow teachers to set up activities in which children can explore the commands at their disposal and come to an understanding of certain elements of the mathematics that underlie what the children are attempting to teach the little 'creature' to do. This does not mean that a totally unstructured child-centred approach should be taken when using robots. Teachers must have clear objectives for the learning that they would like to take place. The task set will lead children to ends determined by the teacher, having made use of particular ideas and instructions on the way. Certainly exploration and experimentation will form a large part of what children do in these situations, but this does not mean that you should not have made some carefully targeted plans.

Once children have become familiar with the basic means of controlling the robot, it is possible to focus attention on a particular mathematical idea, for example problem-solving activities involving the setting up of angles that allow the children to focus on a robot's turns and on recognising the relationship between different sizes of turn, perhaps considering the relationship between the numbers used to complete turns. Or, perhaps at a less advanced level, by considering the number of times the key pad that indicates a turn of 90^0 needs to be used in order to make the robot turn a full circle.

There are many inter-related ideas that children will experience when working with a floor robot. Shape, angle, estimation, rotation, counting, adding and subtracting can all feature in the tasks set. Notions of sequence become very important, and thinking logically at a sophisticated level can be developed in this way. Sometimes the most striking feature of this work is the sheer excitement and fun that it generates. The motivation that is generated serves to keep children on task and working hard, and this bodes well for learning. The children also gain immediate feedback if estimates are incorrect, as the robot continues to move as programmed. This kind of equipment offers the opportunity for children to work collaboratively and to discuss specific ways of solving problems set or encountered.

There are a number of different types of robots available, the most common being roamers, pips and pixies. The roamers and pips can operate on the floor although tend to run more effectively on harder surfaces than carpet – carpet can clog the wheels of roamers and then their accuracy fails. Pixies are tabletop robots but they require careful handling. They must not be revved up or dropped from the tabletop as if they were a toy car. This makes preparation for using these robots vital if they are to be successful in supporting the teaching and learning of the mathematics objectives. For pixies, creating a small wall around the table would protect the robot from damage, but it also means that you must be clear about the rules associated with using this kind of equipment and convey these to the class. Supervision needs to be considered depending upon how many robots you have access to.

The following is an extract from a lesson plan, using a roamer as part of a mathematics lesson with Year 1.

Objective	Vocabulary list
That most children will be able to make and identify a full and half turn; that the more able children will begin to understand a quarter turn as a right angle.	turn full half shape

Teaching activity

Mental/oral starter

Use a Mexican wave format to build children's confidence in counting on and back in 5s and 10s.

Main activity

Organise the children into a circle. Ask a child to come into the centre of the circle and ask them to turn. How far did they turn? Discuss starting position and finishing position. Was it a full or a half turn? Ask a different child to make a different turn and then ask the same questions. Make the children aware that a full turn brings you back to where you started and a half turn leaves you facing the opposite way. Ask each child to do a full and half turn.

Introduce activities

Group 1 – working on roamer with teacher support, looking at quarter turns as right angles.

Groups 2/3 – making the turning machine record what the shape looks like after a full and a half turn. Extend to turning different shapes.

Group 4 – turning shapes and recording what they look like after a half a turn, with the support of a helper.

Plenary

Look at turning different shapes. What happens when you turn a circle? Put a dot on the circle, then ask if the children can tell that it has turned?

Calculators

By the end of Key Stage 2 children are expected to know when it is appropriate to use a calculator or not and to be able to demonstrate this in the National Tests paper, where they are allowed to use calculators. The NNS has produced a video for training purposes to show how children do not always know how to use calculators efficiently whilst they are undertaking their mathematics National Curriculum Test questions.

There are two main issues with calculators – the technical skills of how to use the calculator and their use in mathematics. For the first, giving a calculator to each child and using an overhead alongside can support skills acquisition. For the second, children need to be given opportunities to use calculators appropriately in a range of lessons and not just to check answers. Calculators can be very useful in enabling children to carry out lengthy calculations quickly in order that the teaching focus can be on the underlying mathematics rather than the calculations. For example, children can be asked to work out percentages on the calculator quickly so that the focus can be on the relationship between the outcomes and on a discussion of the patterns occurring. Another example is for the children to use the *constant function* to explore number patterns in multiplication tables.

ACTIVITY

Plan and teach two different lessons using calculators. The first should focus on teaching the technical skills required, and the second should use calculators as an aid to rapid calculation to support the teaching and learning of mathematics. These may be two very different style lessons. In the first, particularly in Key Stage 2, you may find it helpful to look at the paper for the National Tests that allows calculators in order to see the issues involved. In the second lesson, focus on how the calculator enables the children to pay more attention to the mathematics rather than to ways of calculating.

Digital cameras

Although digital cameras rely on a computer package to enable the pictures to be seen and manipulated, we will consider their use here as a computer peripheral. There is not an obvious and direct link between photography and mathematics, but creative teachers have been able to forge worthwhile connections that serve to enhance the overall experience of the learners and to motivate them to engage with their work at a high level. This can best be illustrated with two short examples.

Working on a broad-based topic related to shapes and numbers and the local environment a class of Year 6 children were given the task of setting up a 'Village Maths Trail' which could be used by classes lower down the school. The idea was that the older children would benefit from the work by seeking out numbers, shapes and patterns in the village and combining them into an interesting set of challenges aimed at a particular, younger, audience. As it transpired, a set of very different trails following different routes around the village were developed and used endlessly by generations of six- and seven-year-olds at the school.

The Year 6 children went out in small groups and found examples of mathematics in the vicinity, for example:

- a cartwheel built into a garden wall;
- regular patterns in brickwork in the next wall along;
- circular and rectangular iron drain and manhole covers;
- various configurations of panes of glass in different-sized windows and in a telephone box;
- distances on road signs;
- speed limits;
- triangles, circles and rectangles on road signs;
- odd and even house numbers.

The Year 6 children photographed every example that they came across; once back in the classroom the trail was constructed. At each stopping point on the trail, a short task was set; the older children, with just a little guidance, devised these tasks when needed. Some of the tasks were observation; some relied on making comparisons with photographs and reality (it was possible to alter the images in some cases); some relied on a simple level of calculation – return journeys, for example; some relied on shape recognition; and some on creativity of one sort or another. The end product for the Year 6 children was a village tour 'Guide Book'. This included a map of the route to take and a set of village challenges. Each challenge was accompanied with appropriate and relevant photographs to give help and interest.

Even though the creation and completion of the trail was not totally reliant on the use of a digital camera, it did serve to improve the quality of the work in a number of ways. Back in the classroom, having access to materials that showed the location of artefacts seemed to make the work of devising the challenges more straightforward than if memories or sketches had been relied upon.

The second example is based upon a similar idea. A series of gates was chosen by a group of children and photographed. In pairs the children chose a gate – a garden gate, a farmyard gate, a tennis court gate, etc. In pairs they also took measurements of the gates, which were added to sketches. In school the work on scale that had been introduced was further developed, and accurate scale drawings of the gates were produced. This was not the end of the work; the gate photographs and the scale drawings were then used to help the pairs of children to produce a set of Logo procedures that would draw the gate on screen.

This work took a long time to complete as the number of computers available limited the amount of time that could be spent on it. However, the level of motivation remained high and the final products, and the learning that took place, certainly justified the time and effort involved. The resulting display in the school foyer proved of immense interest to both children and visitors. Again, the digital camera was not central to this work, but added an immediacy and flexibility that would otherwise have been missing. The children's ICT capability was developed in this work as in the first example. A detailed account of some initial work with gates and Logo can be found in Pritchard (1997).

Video cameras

Video cameras can be used in two ways, first to collect images (as with the digital camera) and second to video children working. The second use requires parental agreement under the protection of children acts. Using a video camera in this way can be useful if the class is working on problem solving. The recording can be reviewed in the plenary phase of a lesson to discuss the problem-solving strategies used. Of course, to video your own teaching in order to review your teaching strategies is a good method of professional development at any stage.

Television

Educational broadcasting has developed to the point where there are some exceptionally good programmes available to schools. Initially, making arrangements to have a class sitting ready for a live broadcast was at times difficult, and teachers would then have to hand over the progress of the lesson to the programme makers. This is, of course, no longer the case since the use of video recording has become widelspread. It is possible to buy the programmes on video cassette to avoid the risk of missing the broadcast time (which is sometimes in the early hours of the morning). Once a recording is available, the control of the progress of the lesson rests with you. You are able to stop and start the programme at will, in order to question, clarify or re-run sections as necessary.

The medium of television is now matched by some of the possibilities offered by computer technology, but the shared experience of a television programme, and the exceptionally high production values and educational content which most display, are something which can be put to very effective use. Children are very used to the fast moving images that make up a good proportion of the broadcast output. The ability to follow and to understand what is happening in an adventure cartoon can be put to use in more formal contexts; of course, the best educational programmes are not too much like the break-neck speed of cartoons, but the medium is the same. Another feature of some good programmes is the use of presenters already known to the children; this can have beneficial and motivating effects.

You do need to become familiar with precisely what is available. This can be a time-consuming process, but will prove to be worthwhile. Publicity tends to be good, and summaries of particular series give important details relating to both the National Curriculum and the NNS.

Another aspect of television, which is often overlooked, is the teletext service provided by the main terrestrial channels. Both Ceefax and Oracle are full of real and up-to-date data that can be accessed and used in lessons. Often the concern that teachers have about 'real' data is that the numbers become unwieldy, and cause difficulties with calculations or in understanding the answers when they run to several decimal places. The use of calculators, spreadsheets or databases can alleviate these problems. The use of real data collected from a real medium can both be more interesting for children and serve as a motivating factor in their work.

ACTIVITY

- Look at the television networks' resources for teaching mathematics — many of the programmes are available on video, which make them more flexible for teaching purposes. Make a list of the resources that are available for your chosen age range.
- Plan and teach a lesson using a television programme as one of the resources. What difference did the use of the television make to the lesson? Did you watch the whole programme or did you select parts for specific phases of the lesson? What was the effect on your assessment of learning against the objectives?

Audio recorders

There are few commercially-produced audio resources available now unless you want a rap for reciting the times tables. Using audiotapes with a whole class may not be your first choice, but for group work or for individuals there can be clear advantages. For children with dyslexia, for example, questions pre-recorded on a tape provide support in accessing the same work as the rest of the class but without the need to read the questions or have a reader available. Taped questions also promote listening skills. Children could record questions for others to answer either in the same age group or for younger children. Another possibility is to record clues for a maths trail for a group to use around the school as part of the daily mathematics lesson.

Overhead projectors

OHPs are increasingly used in schools, partly as a result of the introduction of the National Literacy Strategy. However, they can also be used to great effect in the daily mathematics lesson. Simply producing a National Curriculum Test paper question on an overhead transparency can assist you in focusing discussion about how you would answer the question, highlighting key vocabulary, and providing practice for Year 6 children. As a direct result of the greater use of OHPs in schools, manufacturers of mathematics resources have begun to put together specific packs of materials for use with an overhead projector. At Key Stage 1, packs include: counters, number squares, number grids and clocks; at Key Stage 2 packs include: protractors, clocks, number grids, number squares.

The following is an extract from a mathematics lesson using the OHP as a resource for teaching Year 3 children about subtraction of a number in the teens from another two-digit number. Think about the information given here; what else you would want to be able to use in this part of the plan? What would you do differently and why?

Objective
Subtraction of teens number from a two-digit number.

Oral/mental starter
Give the children two numbers and ask them how much had been subtracted from the first number to get the second number.

Children
Provide answers to how much was being subtracted from a given number.

Introduction to the main activity
Display a hexagon that has a two-digit number at each point and a one-digit number inside it on the board. Ask the children to name the shape, then ask them to subtract the number within the hexagon from a number of their choice from those at the points of the hexagon. Repeat, but subtracting 10. Remind the children of place value knowledge and then repeat the subtraction with a two-digit number. Use a number square to demonstrate counting back.

Subtract numbers from within the hexagon from a number on the outside. Discuss methods used to make the calculation.

Then place tens and units wooden apparatus on the OHP. Write a subtraction on the board that involves subtracting a teens number from a two-digit number. On the OHP, demonstrate removing the tens and then the units. Ask the children to model this method using the apparatus on the OHP.

Suggest how many tens need to be removed and then how many units.

OHPs can also be used with overhead calculators. If these are the same kind as the calculators the children are using, then a clear opportunity to demonstrate and train the class how to use the calculator efficiently is presented.

Interactive whiteboards

The interactive whiteboard is used in conjunction with a computer. It can be used to project an image onto the surface of the board and allows you to work with programs like Logo and use a pen like a mouse on the board. You can work with specific software designed to make use of the features of a whiteboard. Writing with the pen can be turned into typed text on its surface – this takes practice to be able to see what the tolerances are for styles of handwriting.

The pen can be used to highlight items on the board for:

- underlining key vocabulary much as you would using an OHP;
- circling specific parts of a calculation or pattern; this could be a scan of children's work upon which to focus discussion;
- demonstrating written methods of calculation;
- writing statements about specific events, such as their probability;
- marking hands on clock faces on the resource backgrounds available in some programs for use with whiteboards;
- marking patterns on number squares showing odds and evens, multiplication patterns and prime numbers;
- highlighting the shapes in pictures taken with a digital camera.

The possibilities for teaching with an interactive whiteboard depend upon whether it has back or front projection. With front projection, one key issue for the teacher and children working on the board is that they stand between the projection and the board, creating a shadow on the board. This makes it difficult to see what you are doing without practice. Back projection, at present the more expensive option, means that you can see clearly what you are doing.

 Summary of key points

In this chapter you have looked at the potential uses of ICT equipment, which goes further than just computers, and its use to support the teaching and learning of mathematics objectives.

- **ICT includes a variety of equipment that can be employed to teach learning objectives.**
- **The effective teaching of mathematics makes appropriate use of ICT in all its forms.**
- **The use of ICT requires careful preparation and planning.**

FURTHER READING

Ainley, J. (1996) *Enriching Primary Mathematics with IT*. London: Hodder and Stoughton.

BECTa: a source of information about new technologies available to schools. www.becta.org.uk/technology/infosheets/index.html

Fox, B., Montague-Smith, A. and Wilkes, S. (2000) *Using ICT in Primary Mathematics: Practice and Possibilities*. London: David Fulton.

DfEE (1999) *Calculator Activities: National Numeracy Strategy*. Available from www.standards.dfee.gov.uk/numeracy

DfEE (2000) *Guide for Your Professional Development: Using ICT to Support Mathematics in Primary Schools*. London: DfEE.

Sharp, J., Potter, J., Allen, A. and Loveless, A. (2000) *Primary ICT: Knowledge, Understanding and Practice*. Exeter: Learning Matters.

Shuard, H., Walsh, A., Goodwin, J. and Worcester, V. (1991) *Primary Initiatives in Mathematics Education: Calculators, Children and Mathematics*. London: Simon and Schuster.

5 Managing ICT in primary mathematics

Introduction

As part of your continuing professional development (CPD) you will, after your NQT year, be taking on responsibility for subject leadership. The relationship between the Professional Standards for QTS and CPD is shown in 'Teachers' Standards Framework' (DfES, 2001c). This maps the Standards that currently exist and the expectations they present. The framework summarises the main elements of each of the standards under ten dimensions of teaching and leadership within a school.

- Knowledge and understanding.
- Planning and setting expectations.
- Teaching and managing children's learning.
- Assessment and evaluation.
- Children's achievement.
- Relations with parents and the wider community.
- Managing own performance and development.
- Managing and developing staff and other adults.
- Managing resources.
- Strategic leadership.

National standards for subject leadership

Subject leaders provide professional leadership and management for a subject to secure high quality teaching, effective use of resources and improved standards of learning and achievement for all children (DfES, 2001c). These standards are in five parts.

- Core purpose of the subject leader.
- Key outcomes of subject leadership.
- Professional knowledge and understanding.
- Skills and attributes.
- Key areas of subject leadership (TTA, 1998).

In this chapter, we will look briefly at the role of a curriculum co-ordinator and how the co-ordinator might develop and monitor the use of ICT in the teaching and learning of mathematics. ICT is one of the resources for the effective teaching of mathematics, but the technical skills and knowledge required and the access to the hardware that is needed make developments in its use more difficult to implement. There are three ways to look at the co-ordinator's role: first the mathematics co-ordinator has to integrate the requirements of ICT in mathematics; secondly, the mathematics co-ordinator may also be the ICT co-ordinator in a small school and so fulfil both areas of responsibility. Third, the ICT and the mathematics co-ordinators must work together on the integration of ICT into mathematics teaching and learning.

The role of the co-ordinator

The role of any co-ordinator includes the following:

- auditing resources and expertise in the school;
- maintaining resources;
- budgetary responsibility for resources;
- monitoring teaching and learning;
- supporting colleagues – subject knowledge;
- supporting colleagues – pedagogic knowledge;
- contributing to the school development plan;
- integrating ICT;
- integrating assessment policy;
- integrating special educational needs policy;
- integrating gifted and talented policy;
- integrating inclusion policy.

We will now consider each of these areas of responsibility in turn.

Auditing resources and expertise in the school

Your audit should include where the school is now, and a realistic summary of the strengths and areas for future development, focusing on the following areas:

- teaching and learning mathematics with ICT;
- children's attainment and progress;
- teachers' subject knowledge and professional development – this will obviously include the co-ordinator's own knowledge (see Chapter 2 for personal audit);
- hardware resources and software resources.

Maintaining resources

You should carry out an annual review of resources available and their current condition. This review should cover all ICT equipment in its widest possible sense. Software should be stored centrally with back-up copies made in case of disk corruption. Teacher's notes and/or manuals will need to be cross-referenced with the software to assist teachers' preparation, planning and teaching. Lesson plans using ICT in mathematics could be held centrally in an ideas bank that all staff can access.

School website

One of the school's resources may include a school website. This is a window into the school and its ethos, and a means of communicating with the wider school community. Before embarking on creating a website, the school community needs to decide the purpose of the website and establish an acceptable use policy. A good starting point is to look at a few sites and decide what you like and don't like about them. You may wish to consider the issue of how much information about individuals is included on the site. For example, will you include photographs of children, full names of staff, contact telephone numbers? Both BECTa and NgfL have information about the safety of school websites on their own websites (www.becta.org.uk and http://safety.ngfl.gov.uk/schools). You will also need to consider who is going to take charge of the site and update its content.

ACTIVITY

Review a number of school websites in order to start discussions about a website for your own school. Collect information about the web-writing software available to the school through its Internet provider and check how much space is available. Alternatively, review the school's present website. Look at how up-to-date the entries are. How could the monitoring of its content be improved?

Assuming budgetary responsibility for resources

You may have a budget for resources and so be able to plan ahead to purchase specific hardware and software. The budget for hardware is more likely to come from grants as computers, in particular, are still an expensive item for many school budgets. Software can also be expensive if bought on spec. It is worth talking to other co-ordinators in different schools to gain information about specific software and its use in school. LEA advisory staff can also be a source of information about a range of products available. In Chapter 3, different types of software were discussed, both content free and content specific. Liaise with other subject co-ordinators as much content-free software is required in subjects other than mathematics, for example Excel, Word and Logo as well as datalogging equipment.

Monitoring teaching and learning

Follow the guidance in the school's monitoring policy. There will be times when you will need to observe the use of ICT in mathematics teaching throughout the school to evaluate its effectiveness, and to discuss this with your colleagues. You may also need to look at medium- and short-term planning to monitor the use of ICT in the daily mathematics lesson, as well as reviewing children's work and their records, to create a holistic picture of the teaching and learning of ICT in mathematics.

Supporting colleagues – subject knowledge

It may be that demonstrating the use of ICT either in your own teaching or after school would be the most effective way to assist in increasing your colleagues' subject knowledge.

When the support needed is related to the mathematics underpinning the use of specific ICT, this may not be the best way forward. The mathematics and ICT may need to be separated initially and then brought together at a later stage. For example, if a colleague needs support in the use of spreadsheets including the use of formulae, some time may need to be spent working on formulae before looking at how these translate very specifically in their use in spreadsheets. The latter will depend partly on the package being used.

ACTIVITY

Plan to work with one colleague to support their subject knowledge, which may focus on their knowledge of ICT and/or mathematics related to ICT. Discuss your plan in advance with your chosen colleague and negotiate the focus of the subject knowledge. Evaluate the process and use this to plan work with another colleague.

Supporting colleagues – pedagogic knowledge

You can start supporting colleagues in two different ways. If you feel confident about using ICT in mathematics, you could ask them to observe you teach and discuss the lesson afterwards. This can work well particularly if you teach the same or a similar age group. It can be more difficult to make the connections between your practice and theirs if the difference in age range taught is very wide. You will need to be very skilled in keeping the focus on the similarities between the teaching contexts rather than the differences.

You may find the following helpful in agreeing a focus for observing a colleague. It is adapted from the training materials for Leading Mathematics Teachers (LMTs).

As you observe the lesson, focus on the following points. You may not see all of these in one lesson but this is designed to give you a starting point.

As you observe, think about:

- what the teacher will have needed to have thought about and planned in preparation for this lesson, particularly in relation to ICT resources;

- how the teacher shares the objectives with the children at the beginning of the lesson, including any specifically related to ICT;

- how the teacher maintains a suitable pace in the mental/oral phase of the lesson whilst using ICT

- how differentiation is managed, particularly when, for example, all the children are using a computer;

- how questioning techniques are used which focus on the mathematics and on ICT skills and knowledge;

- strategies for involving the children when ICT is used, for example, an overhead projector calculator at the same time as the children use their own calculators;

- how mathematical imagery is developed – for example, trends on graphs in Excel;

- how the teacher makes connections between different areas of mathematics and ICT;

- how the teacher demonstrates the key ideas in the main activity, including the skills for using ICT;

- how the teacher manages the transition between the mental/oral and the main activity, either if one phase uses ICT and the other doesn't, or if both phases use ICT;

- how the teacher manages the transition for the children between whole class work and group/paired/individual work, again depending upon whether the transition includes the use of ICT in either or both phases;

- how the teacher organises the activities to support learning for all children, e.g. differentiation by task, support, outcome, including ICT as a resource;

- what the teacher's role is during this part of the main activity – is the focus on the mathematics or ICT?

- how the teacher ends this phase and moves towards the plenary phase, again depending upon where ICT is used in the lesson;

- what the focus of the plenary phase of the lesson is – does it include ICT?

What questions would you like to ask the teacher about the lesson after the observation? Note them down as you observe.

Another approach is to arrange to work alongside your colleague, specifically supporting the use of ICT in their lessons. This requires, of course, that you are released from your own class in order to carry out this activity. This gives you the advantage of seeing something of their practice so that you will be able to make suggestion about using ICT based on their observed teaching strengths. You will also be able to demonstrate the use of ICT with the age group that your colleague is teaching.

A combination of these approaches may enable a shared dialogue and understanding about teaching and learning in mathematics with ICT for future development. Alternative approaches could include disseminating ideas from courses attended, recommending books to read and courses to attend, discussing lesson planning, and arranging in-service sessions.

ACTIVITY

Plan to work with one colleague to introduce a new piece of software and/or hardware into their teaching. Discuss your plan in advance with your chosen colleague and negotiate the focus of the implementation of the new equipment. Evaluate the process and use this to plan work with another colleague.

Contributing to the school development plan

The school development plan will include planned expenditure on hardware for ICT, training for all staff, written policy reviews and evaluations at short- and long-term planning levels. There will also be decisions to be made about the policy of using the Internet as part of the planned development of ICT. All children must be supervised when using the Internet. You need to advise colleagues that if material appears that is not suitable they must switch off the monitor immediately so that the material disappears from sight. All schools have a provider that has filtering systems, but these can be breached. There also needs to be a development plan for the establishment of a school website if the school makes a decision to have one. A policy that everyone signs up to will need to be formulated, including consistency of use of children' names and photographs, discussed earlier (see page 51). This may be included as an action point on the plan. In addition to the school development plan you will need to establish a policy for the use of ICT within subjects. BECTa have useful information sheets on their website that will assist you in putting together a policy document, and help may also be available from your LEA in terms of a format for such documents.

Integration of ICT

You may be working in a school that has a suite for ICT. Decisions will need to be made about timetabling the use of such a room. With schools increasingly teaching all mathematics in the morning this can create difficulties about the suite's use in the daily mathematics lesson for all classes. If you are not the ICT co-ordinator as well as the mathematics co-ordinator then you will want to discuss any potential plans for the integration of ICT across the core curriculum with the relevant co-ordinators.

Integrating the assessment policy

You will need to take account of the school's general assessment policy. Any decisions about assessment involving the use of ICT in mathematics must focus on the assessment of mathematical skills and knowledge in mathematics lessons, and not ICT skills alone.

Integrating the special educational needs policy

ICT can be used effectively as an additional support for children on the SEN register in the practice of skills in mathematics, or it can allow access to aspects of mathematics that would otherwise be unavailable to these children. It may be necessary to modify the ICT equipment or its use because of specific needs, such as those of a partially sighted child who may need a larger screen for large print or those of a child with motor difficulties who may require a modified keyboard.

Integrating the gifted and talented policy

ICT can support the gifted and talented, allowing them access to challenges that stretch their abilities. For example, use can be made of the Nrich website (http://nrich.maths.org/), which is specifically designed to cater for such children.

Integrating the inclusion policy

This may present difficulties if you have children who are, for example, members of the Plymouth Brethren who do not use technology as it is against their religious beliefs. Decisions in school, together with consultation with members of the community, need to be taken about how such children are to be included in school activities, and given as wide an access to the curriculum as possible.

✅ Summary of key points

- **Subject leadership is part of continuing professional development for all teachers.**
- **The role of subject leader and the development of the subject is linked to the school development plan.**

- There must be a clear relationship between the policy for mathematics and ICT and other general policies within the school.
- There are a number of different ways in which you can begin to work with colleagues on the development of the use of ICT in mathematics.
- There are a number of starting points available to assist you in developing your role as a co-ordinator.

FURTHER READING

Ainley, J. (1996) *Enriching Primary Mathematics with IT*. London: Hodder and Stoughton.

Askew, M. (1998) *Teaching Primary Mathematics*. London: Hodder and Stoughton.

Atkinson, S. (1996) *Developing a Scheme of Work for Primary Mathematics*. London: Hodder and Stoughton.

Briggs, M. (1997) *Your Role as Primary Subject Coordinator*. London: Hodder and Stoughton.

Brown, T. (1998) *Coordinating Mathematics Across the Primary School*. London: Falmer.

DfEE (1999) *Superhighway Safety, Children's Safe Use of the Internet*. London: DfEE.

Field, K., Holden, P. and Lawlor, H. (2000) *Effective Subject Leadership*: London: Routledge.

O'Neill, J. and Kitson, N. (1996) *Effective Curriculum Management: Co-ordinating Learning in the Primary School*. London: Routledge.

Skilling, D. (1989) *Managing Maths in the Primary School*. London: NFER-Nelson.

Stow, M. (1989) *Managing Mathematics in the Primary School: a Practical Resource for the Co-ordinator*. London: NFER-Nelson.

Stow, M. and Foxman, D. (1989) *Mathematics Co-ordination: a Study of Practice in Primary and Middle Schools*. London: NFER-Nelson.

This chapter is divided into four categories of resources and further reading in the following areas:

- subject knowledge – mathematics;
- subject knowledge – ICT;
- teaching resources and books for mathematics and ICT;
- ideas for teaching.

Subject knowledge – mathematics

Askew, M. (1998) *Teaching Primary Mathematics*. London: Hodder and Stoughton.

Duncan, A. (1993) *What Primary Teachers Should Know About Maths*. London: Hodder and Stoughton.

Frobisher, L., Monaghan, J., Orton, A., Orton, J., Roper, T. and Threfall, J., (1999) *Learning to Teach Number: A Handbook for Students and Teachers in the Primary School*. Cheltenham: Stanley Thornes.

Haylock, D. (1995) *Mathematics Explained for Primary Teachers*. London: Paul Chapman.

Hopkins, C., Gifford, S. and Pepperall, S. (1996) *Mathematics in the Primary School: A Sense of Progression*. London: David Fulton.

Joinson, R (2000) *Numeracy: Revision for Adults and Students*. Chester: Sumbooks.

Open University (1998) *Passport to Mathematics (M521)*. Buckingham: Open University Press.

Mooney, C., Ferrier, L., Fox, S., Hansen, A. and Wrathmell, R. (2002) *Primary Mathematics: Knowledge and Understanding*. Exeter: Learning Matters.

Suggate, J., Davis, A. and Goulding, M. (1998) *Mathematical Knowledge for Primary Teachers*. London: David Fulton.

Subject knowledge – ICT

Becta (1999) *From Chalkboard to the Internet: the Internet Starter's Handbook*. London: Becta.

Christ Church University College, Canterbury (1998) *Talking About Information and Communications Technology in Subject Teaching – Primary*. Canterbury: Christ Church College.

De Cicco, E., Farmer, M. and Hargrave, C. (1999) *Activities for Using the Internet in Primary Schools*. London: Kogan Page.

Herring, J. (1999) *Exploiting the Internet as an Information Resource in Schools*. London: Library Association Publishing.

Lachs, V. (2000) *Making Multimedia in the Classroom: A Teacher's Guide*. London: Routledge Falmer.

McBride, P. (1998) *Schools' Guide to the Internet*. Oxford: Heinemann Educational.

Sharp, J. Potter, J., Allen, A. and Loveless, A. (2000) *Primary ICT: Knowledge, Understanding and Practice*. Exeter: Learning Matters.

Thomas, B. and Williams, R. (1999) *Internet for Schools: a Practical Guide for Teachers, Parents and Governors*. Barry: Internet Handbooks.

More general, philosophical interest:

Papert, S. (1980) *Mindstorms – Children, Computers and Powerful Ideas*. New York: The Harvester Press.

Papert, S. (1993) *The Children's Machine – Rethinking School in the Age of the Computer*. Harvester Wheatsheaf.

Teaching resources and books for mathematics and ICT

Ager, R. (1998) *Information and Communications Technology in Primary Schools: Children or Computers in Control?* London: David Fulton.

Ager, R. (2000) *The Art of Information and Communications Technology for Teachers*. London: David Fulton.

Ainley, J. (1996) *Enriching Primary Mathematics with IT*. London: Hodder and Stoughton.

Farmer, M. and Farmer, G. (2000) *Supporting Information and Communications Technology: A Handbook for Those Who Assist in Early Years Setting*. London: David Fulton.

Fox, B., Montague-Smith, A. and Wilkes, S. (2000) *Using ICT in Primary Mathematics: Practice and Possibilities*. London: David Fulton.

Hayes, D. (2000) *Handbook for Newly Qualified Teachers: Meeting the Standards in Primary and Middle Schools*. London: David Fulton.

Jacques, K. and Hyland, R. (eds.) (2000) *Professional Studies: Primary Phase*. Exeter: Learning Matters.

Leask, M (ed.) (2001) *Issues in Teaching Using ICT*. London: Routledge Falmer.

Leask, M. and Meadows, J. (ed.) (2000) *Teaching and Learning Using ICT in the Primary School*. London: Routledge Falmer.

Monteith, M. (ed.) *IT for Learning Enhancement*. Exeter: Intellect Books.

Sharp, J., Potter, J., Allen, J. and Loveless, A. (2000) *Primary ICT: Knowledge, Understanding and Practice*. Exeter: Learning Matters.

Smith, H. (1999) *Opportunities for Using ICT in the Primary School*. London: Trentham.

Pritchard, A. (2000) *education.com: an Introduction to Learning, Teaching and ICT*. London: ATL.

Somekh, B. and Davis, N. (ed.) (1997) *Using Information Technology Effectively in Teaching and Learning*. London: Routledge.

Wegerif, R. and Scrimshaw, P. (1997) *Computers and Talk in the Primary Classroom*. London: Multilingual Matters.

Ideas for teaching

Professional journals

Mathematics Teaching (published by the Association of Teachers of Mathematics).

MicroMath (published by the Association of Teachers of Mathematics).

Mathematics for Schools (published by the Mathematics Association).

Microscope (published by Micros and Primary Education).

InteracTive (published by Questions Publishing Company).

Online information

Website evaluation

Teachers, and up to a point children, should be aware that 'all that is on the Internet' is not necessarily good. The obvious examples of this need not be explored here, but at a more subtle level there are some educational sites that are good, and some that are not. To some extent, this might be considered as a subjective notion, but it is important that the worth and validity of a website should be considered before it is used, especially if it is to be used by children. General guidance on the evaluation of websites is available from reputable sources, for example, DfEE (1999).

Simple clues found on a website can tell the user a lot. Since most of what is to be found on the Internet is attempting to sell us something, it is as well to be vigilant and to spot not only the obvious adverts but also the less obtrusive hints found, for example, in the address. '.gov' indicates a governmental site; '.ac.uk' indicates a site located in a British university; '.co' and '.com' tell us that the site is commercial and '.org' is usually a non-profit making organisation. There are many others, too. Most Internet providers will give space free to anyone who registers and so anyone can post absolutely anything on their own website.

Teachers should, and children should be encouraged to, ask questions about a site,

- *Authority.* Who has written the information? What is the authority or expertise of the author? Are there contact details for the author? Who is the publisher of the site?
- *Purpose.* What are the aims of the site? Does it achieve its aims?
- *Audience.* Who is the site aimed at?
- *Relevance.* Is the site relevant to me?
- *Objectivity.* Is the information offered as fact or opinion? Is the information overtly or covertly biased?
- *Accuracy.* Is there any way of checking out what is said here?
- *Currency.* When was the information written?
- *Format.* Does it contain information in the format that I want?
- *Links.* Does the site give me advice/ideas/other choices?

This is not an exhaustive list but will get you started with your surfing journey!

The list that follows includes sites for teachers, e.g. Ofsted, DfES, National Grid for Learning (NGfL) and the Virtual Teachers Centre (VTC). There will be sites from around the world that you can use directly with the children, e.g. online mathematics activities. In addition, there are sites that could support your subject knowledge in mathematics and ICT. If you use American sites, you need to be careful with the amount of written text and issues related to spelling and differences in meaning. Be prepared for children to ask questions about these issues; math is really mathematics, for example.

If we were to recommend just one port of call on the Internet we would suggest the UK government site

www.standards.dfee.gov.uk/numeracy

which deals with standards in general and, in this case, with the use of ICT in the teaching of mathematics.

www.standards.dfee.gov.uk is the UK government's official education site. The link given above leads to the pages relating to numeracy. Also at the same site,
www.standards.dfes.gov.uk/numeracy/publications/
?pub_id=367&top_id=0&atcl_id=0

You will find information about a pack of materials for primary schools, Using ICT to Support Mathematics in Primary Schools. (From this location you will be able to navigate easily around the other resources that are available.) This pack contains a video, a CD with a range of high quality software, a user guide, a guide to professional development, sample lessons using ICT and other associated materials. This package has been available free to schools for some time and many of those who have made use of it are impressed with its contents.

www.open.gov.uk/ofsted/ofsted.htm
The Office for Standards in Education (OFSTED) site gives access to individual school inspection reports and to other OFSTED documents, for example, subject reviews.

www.ngfl.gov.uk/
The National Grid for Learning is a government support network of sites relating to education in all of its manifestations. It is easy to search and holds information, and links to information, almost beyond imagination.

www.becta.org.uk
www.becta.org.uk/technology/infosheets/index.html
The site of the British Educational Communications Technology Agency BECTa (for policies).

www.vtc.ngfl.gov.uk/
The Virtual Teacher Centre (VTC) is a subset of the NGfL, which is more specifically for teachers.

www.enrich.maths.org.uk/mathsf/aims.htm
Mathematics Enrichment Project at Cambridge University.

www.ex.ac.uk/cimt/
Centre for Innovation in Mathematics Teaching based at Exeter University.

www.atm.org.uk/
Association of Teachers of Mathematics (ATM).

www.m-a.org.uk
The Mathematical Association (MA).

www.ambleside.schoolzone.co.uk/ambleweb/numeracy.htm
This is just one example of school website. There are many others that do not take long to find with a little well targeted searching.

Internet sites (subject knowledge)
The Internet is a rich source of many different types of information. Tutorial sites are very common and can be very useful when you feel in need of help in getting started with a new piece of software, or when you are looking for something a little more advanced.

Databases
www.lmu.ac.uk/lss/cs/docs/access/tu-1/tu-1.htm
www.quasar.ualberta.ca/edpy202/tutorial/database/database.htm

Spreadsheet/graphing tutorial
www.ceap.wcu.edu/Martin/tut4.html

An introduction to spreadsheets
www.uwf.edu/~coe/tutorials/technolo/spreadsh/spreadsh.htm
www.quasar.ualberta.ca/edpy202/tutorial/spreadsheet/spreadsheet.htm
www.martinarts.com/tut4.htm

Word-processing
web.mala.bc.ca/etc/resourc/students/wordproc.htm
www.2learn.ca/teachertools/Wordprocessing/wphow2.html

Range of application tutorials
www.cant.ac.uk/title/tutorials/tutorialspdf.htm

Internet sites (classroom use and subject knowledge)
There are many sites on the Internet that offer support for the teaching of mathematics. Below we have listed a selection. Mostly they are from British sites, but we have also included some good non-UK sites. At the end of the list is a sub-section that deals with a source of lesson plans. This list is by no means exhaustive, and some of them may not always be accessible.

www.beam.co.uk/
BEAM (Be a mathematician). Useful site to browse for maths education resources from nursery level to upper primary. It is kept up to date with their current professional development courses and newly released materials and publications. There is also a section that provides links to other sites. BEAM is a mathematics development project for nursery, primary, special and lower secondary teachers and produces a range of innovative resources for mathematics teaching. It also distributes material that support the National Numeracy Project's Framework.

www.mathsyear2000.org/
Site of the Year 2000: Year of Mathematics site, which is still kept fresh.

www.mathsnet.net/
Secondary bias but some very useful ideas and background information for primary teachers.

www.mathsphere.co.uk/
Billed as the number one numeracy website.

www.walsallgfl.org.uk/maths.htm
Walsall Grid for Learning Information and Links for the Maths National Curriculum, National Numeracy Strategy in Walsall, and Walsall Primary Maths Co-ordinators Help File.

www.mathsmaze.co.uk/
Free maths activities, games, puzzles and problems.

www.cadburylearningzone.co.uk/
A colourfully presented website in which children can continue to develop the mathematical skills they are working on in school.

www.4learning.co.uk/
Puzzle Maths and many other useful resources.

www.schoolnet.ca/home/e/resour
The related resources link has a large collection of maths resources from maths news to teaching resources. The Math Forum is the home of Ask Dr. Math, an online maths expert.

www.schoolnet.ca/home/e/
This American site is a helpful resource for 4th to 8th grade students (equivalent to Years 4 to 8), parents and teachers. The site describes and illustrates many maths concepts clearly and in good sequences. It is also good for parents and teachers in areas of probability, integers, percents, number theory, circumferences, perimeter and area.

www.sparkisland.com/
Spark Island learning resources for children, teachers, and parents. Home Spark Island – learning adventures online. A great way for primary-aged children to learn at home or at school.

www.4learning.co.uk/numbercrew/
The Number Crew is Channel 4's television series to support maths teaching to five- to seven-year-olds.

www.counton.org
Count On is the continuation of Maths Year 2000. This aims to make maths accessible and fun, and to help people of all ages to develop the maths skills that they need. Maths Year 2000 builds on the National Numeracy Strategy, which is designed to drive up standards of mathematics in primary schools.

ngfl.northumberland.gov.uk/
Northumberland NGfL Primary Maths Links Teaching and Learning Home Page.

www.wits.ac.za/ssproule/pow.htm
Weekly or monthly problems aimed at various levels.

aleph0.clarku.edu/~djoyce/mathhist
Good starting point for all kinds of mathematics history.

www.m-a.org.uk/
The Mathematical Association. This Association produces several publications and aims to produce good methods of mathematical teaching.

www.westburn.demon.co.uk
Downloadable resources to help develop mental agility and numeracy.

www.liv.ac.uk/~evansjon/maths/menu.html
Maths puzzles, problems and resources for use in schools.

www.tarquin-books.demon.co.uk
Tarquin Mathematics. Books, posters and equipment.

euclid.math.fsu.edu/Science/math.html
World-Wide Web Virtual Library: Mathematics. An extensive catalogue of mathematical links, including electronic journals, mathematics education information, mathematics newsgroups and mathematical software.

www.atm.org.uk
The Association of Teachers of Mathematics serves all teachers of mathematics in primary schools, secondary schools, FE and beyond. This website gives full details of ATM's publications, its activities and its philosophy. It also provides information about its journals and about membership.

smilemathematics.co.uk
Smile Mathematics. Mathematics software, events, books, and a lot more very high quality resources.

el.www.media.mit.edu/groups/logo-foundation/index.html
The Logo Foundation.

www.mathcats.com
Math Cats. A magic chalkboard takes you to interactive maths activities and a maths art gallery. Explore geometry, symmetry, tessellations, probability, Logo programming, animation, conversions and more.

www.gopractice.co.uk
A site where you can sample and order practice books for various school maths tests.

www.archimedes-lab.org
Archimedes' Lab. A huge quantity of maths puzzles to solve and to make, paradoxical problems, tessellations, optical illusions, mazes.

www.teachers.net/lessons
Lots of lessons and activities to use in the classroom supplied by teachers.

www.bbc.co.uk/education/schools/
BBC Schools Online. Useful information for teachers and parents, and activities for children. There are also some useful contacts and links to other sites.

www.WorldOfEscher.com/
World of Escher. This site is dedicated to the great artwork of M. C. Escher. Here you will find essays, images, contests, and products in an easy-to-use layout. Was Escher an artist or mathematician?

easyweb.easynet.co.uk/~iany/patterns/tessellations.htm
Tessellations. Information about tessellations in general – natural examples, examples in art, etc. as well as mathematical. Useful extracts about the work of Penrose and Escher in relation to tessellation.

www.ex.ac.uk/cimt/puzzles/puzzindx.htm
Index of maths puzzles. A list of links to maths puzzles provided by the University of Exeter.

thinks.com/webguide/mathpuzzles.htm
Links to all sorts of maths games and puzzles with clear indication of intended age group.

www.cut-the-knot.com/games.html
Interactive and printable games within TeachersFirst.com

mathpages.com/home/kmath004.htm
Description of palindrome investigations.

www.amathsdictionaryforkids.com/
Maths A to Z – an animated, interactive dictionary for children that explains over 400 common mathematical terms in simple language. Includes definitions, examples, activities, practice and calculators.

www.aplusmath.com/games/index.html
Aims to help children improve maths skills through number-fact games.

www.teachingtables.co.uk
This site hosts great times-table games for one and two players, as well as useful whole class activities and worksheets.

www.math.hmc.edu/funfacts/ffiles/10006.2.shtml
Information about regular solids including properties and diagrams.

www.educate.org.uk
Educate the Children – Primary Education – Lesson plans, worksheets, interactive resources, all linked to the National Curriculum and QCA documentation. For children, parents and teachers.

www.georgehart.com/virtual-polyhedra/vp.html
Pictures of polyhedra (which you can rotate interactively and view from the inside if your browser has the ability to view VRML files) and background information about them.

www.eduplace.com/math/brain/index.html
Brain Teasers for younger people! Three new brain teasers are posted each week on Wednesday with solutions the following week.

www.topmarks.co.uk
Searchable portal of the best educational sites on the Web including maths sites, with resources for children, teachers and parents.

www.pedagonet.com/brain/brainers.html
Develop logic and problem-solving skills.

www.puzzles.com
Although this is a commercial site where you can buy excellent puzzles and games, puzzles.com has many interactive educational games, puzzles, illusions, tricks and toys for you to enjoy and learn from, all freely available on the website.

www.bbc.co.uk/education/megamaths
Maths problems and activities split into two parts, shapes and tables.

www.dupagechildrensmuseum.org
Mathematical problems for young children and primary school children, with extra information on each problem for parents and teachers.

www.ltsn.gla.ac.uk
This is a free on-line statistical resource centre for teachers, which works closely with CTI Mathematics.

www.numeracysoftware.com
Lots of free resources to support maths teaching – numeracy news, numeracy links and free downloads.

www.primarygames.co.uk
Practise maths skills while playing darts and nine other great games. Games have supporting worksheets where appropriate.

www.ex.ac.uk/cimt/
This site aims to provide a variety of materials both for teachers and children, to enhance the teaching and learning of mathematics.

www.funbrain.com/
This site has quizzes and activities for children at graded levels of difficulty. In addition Quiz Lab is a non-commercial resource, which allows teachers to create quizzes for their children online. When the children have completed the quiz the results are emailed to the teacher along with an analysis of the most frequently missed questions.

www.numeracysoftware.com
An excellent site for teachers, which has lots of free resources to download to support maths teaching with ICT.

www.georgehart.com/virtual-polyhedra/vp.html
This is just part of a larger site set up by the sculptor and model maker George Hart. It is full of full of beautiful geometry, and scholarly analysis and classification of the geometric forms. There are sections of classroom ideas and instructions for making models from Zome construction kit.

www.aaamath.com
The site has hundreds of interactive maths lessons covering basic arithmetic. It is an excellent teaching resource for early years through all primary levels.

www.murderousmaths.co.uk
The Official Murderous Maths Site. Details of the Murderous Maths books, extra information, games to play on your computer, links, hints, maths tricks and on-line bookshop.

www.jcutting.freeserve.co.uk
Plot the Robot is a maths activity site involving mental arithmetic and calculator work. When you've got all the right answers, you can construct pictures by plotting them on a grid.

www-groups.dcs.st-and.ac.uk/~history/index.html
MacTutor History of Mathematics. An extensive archive with biographies, index, timelines and birthplace maps, mathematics from various cultures, an index of famous curves, articles and references for further study.

www.softronix.com/
A site where you can download or find out about MSWLogo, a free implementation for Windows of the graphical programming language Logo, including colours and three-dimensional geometry.

www.kidsdomain.com/down/pc/_math-index.html
Lots of free mathematics-related educational downloads.

www.nctm.org/
The home page of the (American) National Council of Teachers of Mathematics, an organisation dedicated to improving the teaching and learning of mathematics.

www.schoolsnet.com
Schoolsnet is an education website based in London providing a range of on-line learning materials including a Schools Guide detailing all the schools in the United Kingdom, an online library and a Web Guide to more than 11,000 of the best educational sites. On the Web Guide, they feature sites of especial interest to parents, children and teachers, in addition to offering a search facility which allows users to locate the most relevant sites for specific homework or classroom enquiries, organised by age and study level.

www.mathsisfun.com
Maths Is Fun contains revision pages, maths games, maths puzzles, off-line activities, a maths discussion board and a monthly maths newsletter. This site contains adverts.

Sources for lesson plans
There are many sites that include a very wide range of lesson plans. Not all of them conform to the type and style that are needed in all schools, but they are a rich source of ideas. The sites under this heading are not the only sites where lesson plans are to be found, but these are probably the most useful:

www.lessonplanspage.com/
A site of lesson plans, lesson ideas, thematic units, and activities.

www.lessonplanspage.com/
Maths lessons on an enormous range of topics related to almost anything imaginable – military activities, calendar events, games and sports and a great deal more.

www.learn.co.uk/
Key stage maths tests in PDF format. Lessons and schemes of work.

www.mountains.freeserve.co.uk/maths.htm
Webwise – Lessons using the WWW. A free collection of lessons plans and ideas designed for primary teachers using the Internet in class.

www.clickteaching.com
Clickteaching: Maths and numeracy resources. Free worksheets, lesson plans and resource ideas and activities for primary school teachers.

DES (1982) *Mathematics Counts* (Cockcroft Report). London: HMSO.

DfEE (1999) *The National Numeracy Strategy: Framework for Teaching Mathematics.* London: DfEE.

DfEE (2000a) *Guide for your professional development: Using ICT to support mathematics in primary schools.* London: DfEE.

DfEE (2000b) *Springboard 5: A catchup programme for children in Year 5.* London: DfEE.

DfEE (2001a) *Springboard 3: A catchup programme for children in Year 3.* London: DfEE.

DfEE (2001b) *Springboard 4: A catchup programme for children in Year 4.* London: DfEE.

DfES (2001c) *Teachers' Standards Framework: Helping You to Develop.* Issue 1 (ref DfES:/0647/2001) Available at www.dfes.gov.uk/teachers/professional_development.

DfES/TTA (2002) *Qualifying to Teach: Professional Standards for Qualified Teacher Status and Requirements for Initial Teacher Training.* London: DfES.

Fox, B., Montague-Smith, A. and Wilkes, S. (2000) *Using ICT in Primary Mathematics: Practice and Possibilities.* London: David Fulton.

Gray, E. and Pitta, D. (1997) 'Changing Emily's Images'. *Mathematics Teaching.* 161 pp 48–51.

Mosely, D., Higgins S. et al. (1999) *Ways forward with ICT: Effective Pedagogy using Information and Communications Technology for Literacy and Numeracy in Primary Schools.* Newcastle: University of Newcastle.

NCET (1997) *Primary Mathematics with IT.* Coventry: NCET.

NGfL/BECTa/DfES (2001) *Impact 2: Emerging Findings From the Evaluation of the Impact of Information and Communications Technologies on Pupil Attainment.* NGfL Research and Evaluation series (available at www.becta.org.uk/impact2).

OFSTED (2001) *The National Numeracy Strategy: The Second Year: an evaluation by HMI.* Available at www.ofsted.gov.uk/public/docs01/nns2ndyear.pdf

OFSTED (2002) *Primary Subject Reports 2000/01: Mathematics* (HMI 356). Available at www.ofsted.gov.uk/public/index.htm

Papert, S. (1980) *Mindstorms: Pupils, Computers and Powerful Ideas.* New York: The Harvester Press.

Papert, S. (1993) *The Pupil's Machine: Rethinking School in the Age of the Computer.* London: Harvester Wheatsheaf.

Pratt, D. (1995) 'Young children's interpretation of experiments mediated through active and passive graphing'. *Journal of Computer Assisted Learning.* 11 pp 157–169.

Pritchard, A. (1997) 'Logo, motivation, and a project about garden gates in a primary classroom'. *British Journal of Educational Technology.* 28(1) pp 5–18.

QCA (2000) *The National Curriculum*. London: QCA/DfEE. Available at www.nc.uk.net/home.html

QCA (2002) *National Curriculum Test 2001: Implications for Teaching and Learning. Key Stage Two Mathematics*. London: QCA. Available at www.qca.org.uk/ca/tests

Sewell, D.F. (1990) *New Tools for New Minds: A Cognitive Perspective on the Use of Computers with Young Children;* London: Harvester Wheatsheaf.

TTA (1998) *National Standards for Subject Leaders*. London: TTA.

TTA (1999) *Using Information and Communication Technology to Meet Teaching Objectives in Mathematics – Initial Teacher Training: Primary*. London: TTA.